The Money Book

The Money Book

*A Layman's Guide
to Survival in Uncertain Times*

Jan Budkowski & Sasha Fenton

Zambezi Publishing Ltd

First published in the UK: 2003
by Zambezi Publishing Ltd
P.O. Box 221 Plymouth,
Devon PL2 2YJ (UK)
Fax: +44 (0)1752 350 453
email: info@zampub.com
www.zampub.com

British Library Cataloguing in Publication Data:
A catalogue record for this book
is available from the British Library

ISBN 1-903065-29-1

Covers & Illustrations:
© 2003-2008 Jan Budkowski
35798642

Reprinted in the UK by Lightning Source UK Ltd
Originally printed in the UK by Antony Rowe Ltd

Disclaimer

This book will be on sale in many countries around the world, and we furnish the following information in order to comply with various regulations.

The intention of this book is to provide general information in regard to the subject matter covered. No book of this size can fully contain or explain all the issues and considerations required for a complete analysis of one's situation. It is sold with the understanding that the publisher and the authors are not engaged in rendering legal, accounting, financial, medical, advisory or any other professional services whatsoever in this book, and cannot be held responsible for the outcome in whatsoever manner the contents may be used. If expert assistance is required in connection with any subject matter covered within this book, the reader is urged to seek the services of a competent professional advisor. Everyone's situation is personal and requires specific, individual consideration on a professional basis in order to achieve optimum results.

No warranties, either express or implied, are made by the authors or the publisher regarding to the contents of this book. It is not intended to reprint all the information that is otherwise available to the authors and/or publisher, but to complement, amplify, supplement and suggest other resources for further consideration. The reader is urged to read all the available material, learn as much as possible about relevant subject matter and to tailor the information to individual needs.

The subject matter of this book does not profess to disclose any form of get-rich-quick scheme, or to be absolutely or categorically effective and accurate.

Every effort has been made to make this book as complete and accurate as possible within the limitations of size and content. However, it is possible that there may be errors, both typographical or in content, and additionally, the contents are not presented as categorical claims by the authors or the publisher. Therefore, this text should be used as a general guide and not as an ultimate source of data on the subject matter concerned. The world of finance is very fast-moving nowadays,.and changes may overtake this book's content rapidly; the reader is advised to check current conditions, laws and regulations while assessing any course of action. Neither the authors nor the publisher are linked to any financial institution.

To the knowledge of the authors and publisher, nothing in this book is in any way illegal or prohibited in the United Kingdom and probably most western-style countries in the world. If any present or future legislation, regulations or any similar factors, whether local, national or international, relevant to the reader prohibit any actions discussed in this book, then the reader is advised to comply with such factors, and assumes full responsibility for compliance accordingly.

The purpose of this book is to educate and inform in a general context. The authors and/or publisher shall have neither liability or responsibility to any person or entity with respect to any loss or damage caused, or alleged to be caused, directly or indirectly, incidental or contingent, by the use or misuse of information contained in this book.

Most of the data mentioned within was current as at the time of writing, towards the end of 2003.

If you do not wish to be bound by the above, you may return this book in good condition to the publisher for a full refund of its selling price.

Jan and Sasha

Pennies don't fall from heaven;
they have to be earned on earth.
Margaret Thatcher.

Sasha's part in this book

My main part in this work is in writing it. I am a well-established writer and I have had well over 100 books published. One other book (which I wrote with Jan, my husband and partner) besides this one has been on the subject of business and finance, and that was specifically for self-employed astrologers and so forth. All the rest have been in the mind, body and spirit genre.

I have been partly or wholly self-employed all my life, often combining a "proper" job in sales, business or clerical work with an artistic, creative or unusual freelance job. Every member of my family owned some kind of business, so I grew up listening to family gossip about financial matters. My first husband, Tony Fenton, ran his own engineering business for many years, and at one point in time he also became involved in buying and selling property in Spain. There were times when I helped out in these businesses and times when I did my own thing. All this has made me far more aware of financial matters than might otherwise be the case. During the years that we have been together, Jan has taught me a great deal about those aspects of money with which I was less familiar. I have used my writing skills and my own store of knowledge in this book, but Jan has contributed his far more detailed financial expertise to every page of this book.

Jan's part in this book

My life started under very uncertain circumstances, because my parents were Polish refugees who landed up, in 1943, in a displaced person's camp in Lusaka in what was then Northern Rhodesia - now Zambia. I was born into a corrugated iron hut in this camp. As soon as my parents found work and began to stand on their own two feet, they moved out of the camp, first into rented property and eventually into a lovely home that they built on what was then the edge of town. Both of my parents always worked - that was the norm, and there were no social security or National Health equivalents.

When I noticed that one of our local banks was looking for staff; I wandered into an interview and took a job as a junior. At the time, I saw this as a temporary measure and it never occurred to me that I would stay in banking for over thirty years. The bank was a South African institution called The Netherlands Bank of South Africa Ltd, or subsequently Nedbank.

I started right at the bottom and worked my way upwards. I also changed countries twice during this time first of all to the then Rhodesia, and later to South Africa. Over a long period of time, I gained first-hand knowledge of the financial hardships associated with economies battered by sanctions, recession, poverty and war.

At one point, I managed credit risk for the bank's Home Loans portfolio and at another I became head of the Internal Credit Audit division. This department audits (analyses the quality of lending) throughout the bank in South Africa. During my time in banking, I dealt with lending in all its forms, whether personal, commercial or corporate. However, I thoroughly enjoyed the time that I spent working in ordinary branches, dealing directly with people, their aspirations and their problems. I dealt with gold miners, diamond cutters, people who owned huge farms, property dealers and the rich and famous of the southern African continent. I was involved with those who dealt in the stock market and those who built churches, synagogues and even Indian temples. I dealt with thousands of ordinary people, including middle-class white, black, Asian and mixed-race people, and also those folk of all colours who had very little money indeed, and who needed to conserve what they had.

My career spanned times of drought, sanctions, recessions, war and large dollops of uncertainty in these countries; from all this past experience, I can see that here in Britain, things are not as secure for ordinary people as they should be.

Sasha and I hope that our different experiences of life and of watching the activities and ups and downs of the people with whom we have come into contact, help us to produce a book that will help you in the very uncertain times that affect us now, and that we feel sure will be around for some time to come.

Contents

1

The Micawber Advice Line

*"Annual income twenty pounds, annual expenditure
nineteen nineteen six, result happiness. Annual income
twenty pounds, annual expenditure twenty pounds ought
and six, result misery."*
Charles Dickens

These famous words of wisdom were uttered by the
feckless Mr Micawber in Charles Dickens's book, David
Copperfield. Mr Micawber had ideas above his station and
he landed in trouble as a result, but this fictional character
was actually based on Charles Dickens' own father. Mr
Dickens senior had a good job at the Navy office but he
preferred a lifestyle beyond his means. Eventually he lost
his job and he was obliged to spend a period of time in the
Marshalsea prison for debt, and it was only the lucky fact
that he inherited a small legacy that eventually baled him
out. Meanwhile, the twelve-year-old Charles Dickens
worked long hours for a pittance in an ink factory, lived

alone in lodgings and took care of himself as best he could. This experience may have been dire, but it served to introduce Charles Dickens to so many of the characters and circumstances that later peppered his wonderful books.

It used to be said in America that the average family has enough behind it to last for three weeks without any money coming in before starting to slide into debt. So, whether you have three weeks, three months or three years worth of money behind you, knowing something about money and how it works will help to keep your head above water.

Who is this book for?

There are already many books around on the subject of finance. Some profess to be intended for the man in the street, yet they present the reader with loads of tables, figures and calculations, which can be very off-putting. Furthermore, these books tend to assume a positive, healthy financial environment, which is not exactly the case in the UK today. Apart from many other signs, and signals, personal debt levels are at their highest levels ever. Property prices have been climbing at up to 30% per annum, a totally unsustainable rate. Our book is aimed at ordinary people who don't know enough about personal finance, but who realise how difficult it is to stay abreast of financial changes, especially in times of uncertainty, such as we are experiencing at present.

This requires quite a different mind set compared to times of peace and plenty. One major feature at such times is the need to keep things simple, while all about you are trying to part you from your savings.

We aim to deal with the subject of money in general terms. If you want to know more about a specific area of finance, we suggest that you read the financial pages that appear in newspapers and financial magazines, find books that are specific to whatever you are looking into. Also search the subject on the Internet, because there is an incredible amount of valuable information on the net nowadays. Many newspapers list the best rates for credit cards, savings, borrowing and mortgages, and these suggestions are good enough for most normal purposes.

Those who wish to play the stock market will need much more immediate information than this, but this book is not aimed at such investors. We have only offered an overview of such things as current tax rules or social security issues, as these are apt to change. In short, this book is for those of you who live ordinary lives but who need to cope with an increasingly complex world in times that might soon prove to be extremely difficult.

Money is an emotive matter

Money means different things to different people. It can range from the means of obtaining basic security and from being debt free to being able to treat yourself to a good holiday or other nice things from time to time. We are not looking at the emotional or relationship implications of money in this book, but simply outlining the mechanics of managing money. We seek to tell you how to spend, save and borrow wisely. We can't make you rich or successful and we cannot prevent catastrophes from happening. However, if we can prevent one person from getting clobbered due to a lack of foresight, we will have accomplished what we have set out to achieve.

If you get nothing else from this book, we urge you to take two ideas on board. The first is to save, and the second is to grasp the difference between *needing* something and *wanting* it; this way, you will either remain debt free, or at least be able to limit the damage if too much uncertainty enters your life.

Who is the best person to look after your finances?

There is absolutely no doubt that the person who will make the best job of looking after your money is you. Some independent financial advisors may give you worthwhile advice, but others may have their eye on giving your money to the company that offers them the best rate of commission. Banking staff want to help you, but they are hidebound by the changing policies of their institutions and the rules and regulations that are locked into their computers. If they are suddenly told to call in an overdraft or not to lend as much as they were allowed to previously, there is little that they can do about it.

The people who want to lend you money at extortionate rates of interest (and this includes many credit card companies) won't care if you struggle for years to pay off these loans. The shops that offer you things that you just can't resist won't look after you when you can't afford to pay your rent or eat properly. Friends, relatives and lovers may mean well, but do they really know what they are talking about? We have even discovered that those who work at the Benefits Agency, both in the past and at present, can give you misleading or completely wrong information.

We have done our best to advise, warn and help you to deal with the financial minefield in what is likely to be a more difficult and dangerous future. We can make suggestions, but at the end of the day, you must do your own research, make your own decisions and take control of your own finances and your own life. We hope that our book helps you to do just this. Below is a dramatic example of how leaving things to chance can go badly wrong.

A king-sized rip-off

Kirk Douglas's second wife was a sensible Belgian woman who had her head well screwed on. A year or two after they were married she decided to look into his financial affairs. It was not long before she was certain that something was very wrong. When she spoke to Kirk about her suspicions, he replied that his wonderfully fatherly financial manager dealt with those things for him - and that he trusted him implicitly. Film stars of his calibre have so much provided for them by their studios that they don't really need money of their own on a day-to-day basis. They frequently leave their financial affairs in the hands of managers, and it is only when they stop working that they start to look into what they have put by, if they do so at all. Needless to say, everything that Kirk had earned in 17 years had been creamed off by his "helpful" financial manager. Kirk soon discovered that the same man had taken Doris Day for every dollar that she had earned in 21 years of hard work.

Well, you may not be on your way to Hollywood stardom, but the fact still remains that the best person to look after your finances and your financial future is you, and you must take control of your own destiny. Sadly, there are still women who are happy to hand over financial decision making to the man in their lives, and while this may work in some cases, it often ends in near tragedy for the woman and her children. Whatever your age and your gender, it is up to you to understand what is going on and to deal with it.

Jan's banker's nose is telling him that the future looks very uncertain indeed and that those who have over-extended themselves could land in real hot water sooner or later. So, get your head around your financial realities now. Start to save and to protect your savings, and you will be better able to cope with job losses, unexpected expenses and other setbacks if needs be. If it doesn't prove necessary, then you will have a nest egg for the future and something that will go towards a comfortable retirement.

Having said all the foregoing, it is worth noting that stingy, miserly people are never really happy. Wives, husbands and children desert them and they end up in a lonely and fruitless old age. If they are lucky, they still have their money to count, but it is amazing how often this is taken away from them, by investments that go sour or expensive houses that crumble around them for lack of care and expenditure. Stingy people tend to look and act unappealing, as all their thoughts are concentrated on their money. So, here - as in everything in life - moderation is the option that is most likely to lead to happiness.

2

Uncertainty

Jan's take on uncertainty

There is much talk lately about the possibility of another recession. We see various reports in the media about job losses, company failures or mergers, directors pulling out massive payoffs after having done nothing of value for their companies, and many other stories of the same kind. The same applies to many other countries within the EU and elsewhere, including the United States. Make no mistake, there are genuine reasons for concern nowadays, but there is not a lot that the individual can do to solve the world's problems.

As the subtitle of this book says, uncertainty is the name of the game nowadays, and the best thing we can do is to take steps to minimise the possible effects of any downturn on our families and ourselves. The uncertainty aspect makes it impossible to predict what will happen - or when and how. However, it is possible to understand the *kind* of things that might happen, and what action we should take. So, let's have a look at a few of the economic problems that tend to affect all of us one way or another.

Inflation

Very basically, this means that money becomes less valuable over time. Either goods become more expensive, or money becomes too easily available – for example, if wages and salaries grow without a parallel increase in productivity. Here is a very simple, exaggerated, but accurate example. Let's say your job is in the manufacture of furniture and you produce one armchair per week. The armchair sells for £100 and your wages are £50 per week. Ignoring all other costs and considerations in our very basic example, the company will make £50 profit per armchair after paying you your wages.

If, over the years, your wages go up until eventually you are being paid £90 per week, then the company is only able to make £10 profit per armchair. Going on another year or two, your wages rise again now reaching £110 per week. Now, the company is actually losing £10 per armchair. If it continues like this, it will run out of money because it has to make a profit to survive. In the same way, if you spend more than you earn, you will also go bust very quickly.

On the other hand, if your productivity (number of armchairs per week) improves, then things are quite different. If some way is found for you to be able to produce two armchairs per week, your wages can easily rise to £110 per week, because now the company is selling two armchairs per week and making £200 per week. This helps to avoid inflation (money becoming less valuable), it keeps you in a job and happy with your income - and it keeps the company solvent.

Naturally, there are many more factors of all kinds involved - is there enough of a market to buy two armchairs per week? Does the style go out of fashion? Do the material and other costs stay reasonable and so on? Nevertheless, as you can see, the basic principle is there.

Recession

Recession is a time when business activity and employment decline, and the possible reasons are many, but it is the effects that we are concerned about here. Banks and other financial institutions begin to feel the pinch, because people have less money to put in the banks, which means the banks have less money to lend,and this being their main trade, they make less profits. So, new schemes and offers proliferate, to tempt you to invest or deposit or one way or another, to put some money in to the institution.

The same applies to shops and retailers in general. Special offers and the like all tempt people to spend some money, but people don't have much of it any more, so they borrow, and you have more problems arising.

You have to cut back your spending ruthlessly if you are to survive through periods of recession. You need to hold on to your job, and you need to save as much as you can. Really, the saving part of this equation is what one should have been doing all along in the good times, because that's when money was available...

Depression

This is the name for a very severe recession, but otherwise basically the same thing.

Deflation

This is an important problem that is worrying a number of countries at the moment. Japan's economy has been subject to deflation for a number of years now. The base rate of interest at the Japanese Central Bank is now zero - that means nought per cent. Some EU countries (like Germany) are in the early stages of deflation, but everyone is hoping that things will improve. Hope is one thing, but what we all should do is realise that we should prepare for the possibility. Similarly, you don't take out life assurance because you expect to drop dead tomorrow, you take it out because uncertainty says that the possibility is there, and it needs to be provided for even if (hopefully) it never does happen.

The last time the world experienced deflation was in the Great Depression, which was seventy–odd years ago. This means that there are very few people around who have actually experienced its effects. It is the opposite of inflation, and what happens is that things become cheaper. They don't become cheaper due to productivity, but because there is less demand. People have less money to spend, so they are forced to buy fewer things. This means that the manufactures can't sell their stocks or release the money that they have tied up in their stocks. They drop their prices to entice people to part with what money they have. "Bogofs" (buy one, get one free), three for two, discounts, special offers, sales and the like, are all the same thing – prices dropping. Much of the time, these inducements are normal, but if you see a strong increase in such offers, then deflation may be in the air.

Another of the effects of deflation is that money becomes more valuable but less available. Loans become harder to obtain, except from loan sharks - and they should be avoided like, well, like sharks! If you don't have enough saved up, then you will need a loan, and that leads you into a trap where you end up needing more and more loans to cope with the escalating amount of interest, yet less money available to repay the loans, let alone to live on.

While loans become more difficult to obtain, there are some that become temporarily much easier - mortgage loans, for example. We heard on the news this evening that there are now about 4,000 different flavours of mortgage loans available. This hardly seems credible, but there we are - an immense number of ways to lend you money... against tangible, safe, security; i.e. your home. How many flavours of unsecured overdraft facilities are there? Mortgages become tighter once there is a certain level of defaults, that starts to hurt the institutions through negative equity. So, the answer here is clear - don't become greedy and get the biggest mortgage you can, don't be fooled into thinking property prices will never come down again.

We pointed out earlier that with inflation, money becomes less valuable, although more available. Deflation means the reverse. *Deflation* means that, more than ever, you must not waste your money or spend it unless it is necessary, and you must save as much as you can. That is the key to surviving such uncertain times.

You will find all sorts of things to tempt you into opening your wallet. That swish new car, the longed for Aga or that lovely lounge suite become very reasonably priced. Don't do it. The retailers want you to spend to stave off closures, but will they help you when you run out of money?

It is interesting that the government appears to be making savings less attractive – for example, with effect from April 2004, ISAs no longer have a tax exemption on dividend income. Does this mean that they want us to keep spending, to keep the economy going? Who knows. Nevertheless, do the right thing for yourself and don't be tempted, because you may need all the money you can find, over the next few years.

Turn unwanted clutter into money, and have fun doing a few boot sales. If you have no use for things and you can get a few quid for them, flog them. Check out the attic, the garage, wherever and be ruthless. Sasha tells me it is good Feng Shui to make your home clear of clutter, so perhaps she has something there too!

Don't be tempted into being greedy. If some bank or other institution offers you a fantastic interest rate or a wonderful investment opportunity, be very careful. Read all the small print or get someone more knowledgeable to check out those tempting opportunities out for you. If it wasn't available when times were good, the chances are that it's more of an opportunity for the institution than it would be for you. They make it sound easy to make money by investing, but that isn't so. It is easy to lose money, and most investors do that regularly by being too greedy and impatient.

Don't go borrowing money from loan sharks and other shady types. Their interest rates and charges are likely to be ridiculously high. I was dumbstruck when I learnt recently that in Britain, there is no equivalent of the Usury Act that I knew in South Africa. Such an Act limits the maximum amount of interest that can be charged by a lender. There is a real case for this kind of regulation - it has come to light recently that some loan sharks are charging, quite legally, rates well above 50% per annum, which is absolutely untenable.

I am well aware of the benefits of self-regulation, freedom of trade and the like, but my motto is moderation. Moderation is always lacking when times get tough, and self-regulation only works in good times. As we have seen recently, bloated payouts, bonuses, horrendous overcharging and other totally unwarranted examples have been features in the news, both in the UK and in the USA.

What can you do to help yourself?

One very, very important thing is to save and invest money to provide a cushion for bad times. By rights you should do this all your working life! Not just when things start to get tough. If you haven't been doing this, start doing something about it right now. And teach your children the same thing so they don't make the same mistakes when they grow up. Bear in mind that in the long run, nobody is really going to care that much about you except you yourself. Whatever politicians and other esteemed authorities say, what tends to happen is quite different. Look at the current pension fiasco, both in the private and public sectors. Look at the railways, the education system and all the other problems today. There is always a reason for passing the buck onto someone else, until everybody is so weary of fighting the issue that they just drop it. Don't rely on anyone but yourself to look after you and your future.

If you can't save much, that's fine, do what you can. Save a few pennies, a few coins, but save *something*. Get into the habit of thinking save, save, save… as you do this, you will find that you can actually save more than you first thought. The important thing is to start now, not tomorrow. Saving creates the right energy and atmosphere for your life to improve. It takes time, so get into it right now. Put down this book, go and find a coin and an old cup or soft drinks can, put the coin in and put the cup or can on a high shelf so that it is out of the way.

Good. If you have done that, you're already on track to get somewhere. Read this book again in two or three years time and you will see that we're not just making a drama out of this savings bit, as it is the most important financial thing you can ever do.

~ Try to make yourself as valuable as possible at work.
~ Minimise the chances of being made redundant.
~ Do what you're supposed to do, don't skive off, don't get a doctor's note about your flu every couple of weeks and don't take two hour lunches. If someone has to be made redundant and the company has a choice, who do you think they will choose? Will they chuck out the productive person or the one who is away watching football on a doctor's note?

~ Don't waste money. Read what we've said elsewhere in this book about the difference between "needing" and "wanting" things.
~ Keep your mortgage and any other loans well within your ability to service and repay.
~ Make it a goal to set aside, as part of your savings plan, at least six month's worth of repayments on your mortgage, loans, and essentials like lights, water, council tax, etc. This means that, even if you do lose your job, you will have at least six months in which to sort out something else.

If this sounds like a daunting goal, then the sooner you start, the sooner you will achieve it. Yes, it is possible. You can do it. If you already have this money set aside, terrific.

Don't ever stop saving, but be kind to yourself, so ensure that you have a little something set aside for a bit of a break - whether it's an evening out, a weekend away, or whatever.

Dodgy investments

I won't list all the negative things that can happen in a recession or during a period of deflation because that can be depressing. You should just plan to be doing the right things all the time, because then you are doing the best you can for yourself and your family. One consolation is that such times tend to be fairly brief. The longest depression in the USA lasted just over three years. All things are temporary – both good and bad times.

There are times when it's best to cut your losses and run, and if you're into the stock market, this is important. You may find it best to sell uncertain shares, even if you make a loss on them. Use your common sense and take advice before doing so, but be prepared to take a knock for the sake of the long-term view.

Bonds may be a good idea as an alternative to shares, but this kind of investment depends on timing. If you're reading this in the middle of a major stock market crash, then bond prices will already be prohibitive. There are also risks involved with bonds – they are only as safe as the issuer, and we have already seen some very big corporations bite the dust in recent years. If it looks like recession or deflation are looming, then most likely you should play safe.

Stay out of the markets and keep your money in nice, safe cash, in a nice, strong bank – not just any bank but a good, sound bank. Don't bother with newcomers offering great rates, but just stick with the reliable, steady institutions. Beware if Internet banks. Even if they are perhaps sound, in the event of a crash, you'll find that everybody is clamouring to get their money moved and the website will be totally clogged up and unusable, leaving you stuck. For those of you who may have tried to sell shares during a past stock market crash, remember how difficult or even impossible it was trying to phone your broker... well, multiply that by a hundred if you're trying to do it on the internet!

Only this morning that I was trying to move some money between our accounts – not in an Internet bank as such but just by using the Internet. Well, it took me over an hour to do the simple transfer that normally takes a few minutes. For some reason, the bank's website was either very busy or had some kind of malfunction. It is best to be able to visit an earthly branch where you can get hold of an actual human being rather than an engaged tone.

Property

Property is a great alternative to the stock market, right? Well, at times, property can be terrific. There are people who have made an incredible amount of money during the property market spree over the past few years. Hopefully, they will have now taken their profits out and invested them elsewhere, as the incredible property price rises are likely to have topped out. Nothing lasts forever, and there are good times and bad times for any kind of investment. The trouble with property in bad times is that it is not liquid, so you can't get your money out quickly when you need to. In fact, when you need to, probably everybody else needs to as well…and with everybody trying to sell up, the only thing that can achieve a sale is to drop your price radically. Sometimes even a 50% drop is not enough. Sometimes, you can't give it away!

Remember that whenever the markets drop badly, property prices will drop as well. So if you expect a stock market crash (we can't predict timing on that), be aware that you should already be out of property investments.

Don't overextend your mortgage. Property prices have scaled the heights recently and your home may be worth an astonishing amount of money now. Don't assume that entitles you to remortgage up to the hilt again. What is important is whether you can keep up your mortgage repayments, and if you needed to sell your house, whether it would sell for more than your outstanding mortgage.

During really black times, there is one strange reason where a remortgage might be useful, and that is to allow you to put money aside, to ensure that you can keep up mortgage repayments for a couple of years if needs be. This may sound crazy, but it can be very important to be able to access money for critical things like mortgage repayments. If you have little or no savings set aside, this may be the one valid reason for increasing your mortgage.

The great antiques road show

Don't get into collectibles. In bad times, the only thing of value in a gold coin is the gold, not the rarity. If you happen to have inherited a collection of some kind, that is all well and good, but don't be misled into buying collectibles as investments for safety in hard times. Naturally, if you are a genuine expert, that may be an exception. Just make sure you aren't the only one who considers you to be an expert...

Annuities

If you are nearing retirement and having to give thought to your pension, then consider carefully which insurance company you place your annuity with. Where personal pension plans are concerned, you normally have a choice as to which organisation will arrange and pay you your pension annuity. It does not have to be the same organisation into which you paid your pension premiums all along. It is up to you to decide where to place your pension monies, and what kind of annuity you want to have. Here again, we understand that there are now over 1,600 flavours of private pension schemes on tap. The institutions are doing whatever they can to draw your business in their direction. What are they doing? They are trying to survive. What should you do? Try your best to survive. Don't think loyalty, that is history. Loyalty must be a two way thing, and if the new rules of the game are that it's ok for you to be enticed away from one institution to another, then make it your business to take the best deal for you from another institution, if that is necessary to fulfil your needs.

There is a range of options and you should get these explained to you. Use an insurance broker and get someone from a different insurance company to talk to you, in addition to the company that is administering your pension premiums. Your pension plan company will naturally want you to stay with them, but this is not necessarily the best option for you. Sometimes you can get up to a 30% better deal elsewhere, and when you consider that you *cannot* change your mind after you have chosen an annuity and its provider, you can see why you shouldn't automatically leave things for your current insurance company to handle.

One thing to remember with annuities is that, in the health questionnaire that is always required, the opposite applies compared to when you apply for a life policy – if you have some serious disease that may shorten your life expectancy, some insurers will give you a better quote for your annuity! The reasoning being, of course, that they may not have to pay you for as long as would be the case if you were as strong and healthy as a horse. Smoking is one of the attributes that may improve your quote, so it is better to be honest about any afflictions you may have. They will check with your doctor anyway, so it is always better to be honest with your details.

The other important thing is to choose a strong, well-run insurer, not just one that gives you the best quote. Remember that your annuity is only as safe as the insurer – so if they go bust, so does your annuity, it isn't made of cast iron…

Sasha's take on uncertainty

In financial terms, uncertainty means that taxes and interest rates rise, property prices may zoom down and jobs and money may be hard to find.

What is a crash?

A crash means that shares in public companies that are quoted on the stock exchange lose a large proportion of their value. From the start of the millennium until March 2003, the stock market has not so much crashed as *slid* downward, with shares losing around 37% of their value in that time. The market has been picking up slowly since then, but the global outlook is not good - and what happens in one country can swiftly affect what happens in others, especially if there is little cushion in the economy.

How on earth can such global and high-level economics affect you? If you are like the majority of the population (including the two of us), you are hardly likely to spend your day gambling on the stock exchange or have "loads-a-money" to splash around. You are probably buying your home on a mortgage, you may have a bank loan or some other kind of loan, you may have hire purchase for some large item or perhaps finance for a car, and you may have some outstanding credit card debt. You work, you have family attachments and you live an ordinary life. You buy what you need (and sometimes a few things that you don't need), you like to have at least one nice holiday a year and you try to put some money aside for a rainy day.

The problem is that the stock market is not so separate from the ordinary person's financial life that it has no effect on us. It is a means of both raising money for and measuring the performance of the largest companies and industries in our country. If these are doing well, jobs and money will filter down throughout the economy. Large companies buy components from smaller ones, and the people who are employed use the services that others supply. If money starts to become short in one sector, it will affect others. Older readers may remember what happened to those towns that depended upon the old "smoke-stack" industries such as coal and steel. Younger readers may have seen that wonderful film "The Full Monte" which was based in Sheffield – a city whose former wealth was based on steel and engineering but which lost the means of employing and feeding its population. If "male" jobs such as manufacturing go to the wall, "female" jobs, such as clerical work, shop work and even cleaning go with them. After all, there will be nobody to employ typists, nobody to buy goods in shops and no factories or offices to clean.

Even if our country is doing well, it still needs to trade with the rest of the world, and we have to sell goods to others in order to generate inward investment from other countries. Much of this has come from the much-despised European Union over the past few decades, while other money comes from sales to America, the Far East, the old

Commonwealth countries and elsewhere. If books and magazine articles written by Sasha can (and do) turn up in such weird places as Bali and Borneo, someone must be importing them.

If we all buy less, go out less and make things last longer, the commercial life of our country starts to suffer. However, on a personal level, we would be crazy to rush out and buy luxuries just because it is good for world trade. There comes a point at which ordinary people like us have to say, "Stuff world trade, I need to look after myself and my family!"

The ordinary person's I Ching

You have probably heard of the ancient Chinese divination system called the I Ching. The word "Ching" means book and the "I" bit stands for something like "*advice on how to cope in catastrophic times*". The I Ching gives 64 separate pieces of advice that can be linked to any of life's dilemmas. The origins of the I Ching reach back to the end of the last Ice Age, and the Chinese people have certainly lived through many catastrophic times since then. Hopefully, the current global downturn may not turn out to be a catastrophe, but what if some kind of catastrophe does occur? Well, in case it does, perhaps take a few tips from this mini version of an "*I Ching according to Jan and Sasha*".

Jan and Sasha's I Ching

~ Plan ahead in case hard times are around the corner.

~ Put your money into boring places such as a high street bank or a really solid building society.

~ Keep some spare cash in a safe place. In the words of Jan, "this time around, when times are hard, cash is king!"

~ If you are rich, read the section in this book on investing in gold.

~ Don't borrow money for things that you can do without.

~ If you think there is something that you really will need to buy in the near future, wait for prices to fall and then buy it.

~ Ensure that your pension plans, insurance policies and so on are with reputable and safe companies (not with Equitable Life, for instance). If they are not, then it may be best to wind them up, accept the penalty that comes as a result of this and move what's left of your money elsewhere. As always - get sound professional advice before jumping to major conclusions.

~ Sell anything that you don't need – this can mean anything from making a trip to a top auction house to taking a pitch at the local boot sale.

~ If you are running a business that is not getting anywhere, sell it and get a job.

~ Don't handle everything yourself, tell your loved ones about your worries and fears and involve them in your plans.

~ If older members of your family have poor investments, give them this book to read.

~ If there is some piece of equipment that you think you will need in order to earn or make money, buy it now while you still can. We are thinking about such things as a computer, a sewing machine and a run-around car.

~ Don't buy anything that you don't actually need.

~ Don't gamble with stocks and shares.

~ Don't buy a house that stretches your finances to the limit.

~ Don't take a large mortgage if there is any chance that house prices will fall. If you have to sell the house later, you will still have to pay the remaining part of the mortgage.

~ If you still wish to invest, buy unit trusts that invest in a spread of things - including the stock market, then keep the investment going over a long period of time (at the very least, for five years).

~ Don't buy antiques and other such stuff as an investment.

~ If you fancy a caravan holiday, rent the van rather than buying it. Alternatively, buy an old one, put it in the garden and use it as an inexpensive extension to your house!

~ Don't commit yourself to paying for private education for your children, use tutors at home in addition to state education.

~ Don't have a huge wedding and expensive honeymoon if you have to borrow money for the purpose.

~ Don't assume that the government, social security or other official bodies will look after you if things get really bad.

~ If you want to have a baby, go ahead. We know you won't be able to afford one, but who cares? Babies are lovely and if you are canny, you will be able to buy 90% of the stuff they need second hand or at your local boot sale.

There are probably other ideas that we have not thought of, but a bit of common sense and thought on your part, allied to communicating with all generations in your family could avert disappointment at best and the I Ching of catastrophe at worst.

3

Banks and Banking

*"Bear in mind that all companies, financial institutions
and corporations have only one ultimate responsibility,
and that is to their shareholders!"*
Jan Budkowski 2003
*"A bank is a place that will lend you money if you can
prove that you don't need it."*
Bob Hope

The local branch manager who knew his clients well is a
vanishing species - if he is not already extinct. Banks have
rationalised by closing small local branches, so now we
have personal bankers, business bankers and computer
systems. Some banks only operate over the Internet. In
many ways these changes work in our favour but not in all.
For example, there was a time when someone from a local
branch would phone to ask a client whose current account
was running into overdraft if he wanted to move some
money across from his savings account. As a general rule,

if a person runs into an unauthorised overdraft now, the bank will send a letter and then charge a hefty fee – regardless of the fact that the client may have plenty of money in another account in the same bank.

Handling money is now more than ever a matter of personal responsibility, but the most vigilant of us can still be caught out. Once upon a time we used a chequebook - and as long as we made a note of what went into and out of an account, it was easy to see where we stood at any point in time. Direct debits and cashpoints are wonderful, but they can sweep money out of a current account and land us with an unauthorised overdraft before we are aware of it. One benefit of being able to use the Internet to access our bank statements is that we can check what is going on and move money around ourselves when necessary. So, it is swings and roundabouts – easier in some ways and more difficult in others.

As you will see in the chapter on savings, there is such a variety of banking services these days that it is hard to keep up. Some organisations specialise in one or two areas of finance while others offer a full range of services. If you are in business you will probably use one of the "big four" high street banks but if you are only dealing with personal matters, you may use any one of a number of institutions.

Loyalty is a two-way thing, and the old ethos of ethics and loyalty to the customer has gone out of the window in today's banking world. Many people open an account at the bank that their parents and even their grandparents used and then stay with that bank for life, while others move around according to their needs. We don't make a case for either course of action, but we suggest that you keep your eyes open and see who is offering the service you need at the most competitive rates.

Even if you have very little money and you fear becoming overdrawn, you can still use a bank. The banking services offered by the post office are becoming more sophisticated, and soon you will be able to use an account there for dealing with benefits. You can open a bank account with as little as £1. You can ask for an introductory account, which may also be called a basic account or a starter account. This allows you to save and spend your own money but not to overdraw. You can even use a cash point card with this account, but it will only allow you to take money out of the "hole in the wall" if you have some in your account. However, there is a tiny buffer zone, so if you can only take £10 out of the machine and you only have £6 in the account, it will allow you to borrow the other four pounds free of charge. This account should pay direct debits for you (which can be a cheaper way of paying for essential services), but you must ensure that you have enough in the account to cover these.

Top tips

Those who have never used a bank and who are intimidated by the thought of going into a bank or who think they will never need to use one, should get the leaflet called "No Bank Account" which is available via the Financial Services Authority, 25 The North Colonnade, Canary Wharf, London E14 5HS. Their website is www.fsa.gov.uk. This covers some of the points that we have raised here and more.

Generally speaking we have avoided recommending one organisation over another in this book, although we sometimes point out those that offer specific services. We ourselves use one of the well-known high street banks for both business and personal matters, and we are glad to report that so far we have received good service.

4

Saving for your Future

Take care of the pence and the pounds will take care of
themselves.
William Lowndes.
One should always put something aside, however little
one earns.
Andrew Carnegie

Savings schemes can encompass anything from a child's
piggy bank to large sums of money. Investments are a
different matter, so we will look at those in another chapter.

If you tuck away ten per cent of the money that comes in
every week, you will end up rich. Even if you can't put this
much away but still save a small amount each week, you
will eventually end up with a nest egg. Later you will be
able to split your savings into different pots for different
purposes. Do this as soon as you receive the money rather
than saving what remains after you have been on a
shopping spree.

Some facts as they are in the UK at the time of writing this book (end 2003)

~ The inflation rate is lower than it has been for decades.
~ Interest rates are low.
~ House prices are ludicrous.
~ Rents are stabilising or even falling.
~ Large items cost much the same as they did several years ago and some cost less than they previously did.

Despite the foregoing, are Sasha and I the only ones who notice that the cost of food is leaping up, despite all the hype about low prices? Some measure of inflation can't be too far over the horizon, but so could *deflation*.

Inflation is easy to understand, as this is what happens when prices rise. Suddenly people can't cope and the Trades Unions start to ask for higher wages for their members. This begins to spiral and soon everybody is short of funds. Deflation means that the value of money is strong but there may not be enough of it available for spending. Very basically, deflation occurs when consumers (i.c. you and us) don't have enough money to spend, so manufacturers and retailers drop their prices in a desperate attempt to avoid closing down. Food is a necessity, so there will always be a market for this, and even in deflationary times the price of food can rise.

Sasha says she is glad that Jan has explained this, because she found it difficult to see why his nice new jacket was so cheap, while the contents of her fridge cost more every week...

In times such as these, the future situation could go in any direction, so it makes sense to put something by. Even putting coins in a piggy bank is better than nothing, although it is not a good idea to keep large sums of money around the house if your living space is not totally private. Jan has always plonked his small change into a pot and this mounts up to the point where we find that he has saved enough for us to have a few days holiday or to buy ourselves something nice.

Jan's words of wisdom

Before we start analysing savings as a whole, Jan wishes to repeat a small section that also appears in the chapter on mortgages, just in case you skip that chapter, so here are a few words of wisdom from Jan…

Many people don't realise that their mortgage can also be their best savings scheme, especially when other schemes offer minimal returns or high risks. How? Well, what you need is a "flexible" mortgage. Different institutions use different names for these, and different terms and conditions but the basic idea is the ability to put extra amounts of money into your mortgage account, and to be able to withdraw this money whenever you need to.

Using this basic example, imagine the effect on your mortgage if you want to put £5,000 into the account and leave it there for a while. This reduces the balance by £5,000 and therefore, your interest charge is correspondingly less. So, instead of your monthly requirement mainly going towards the payment of interest, it is used to reduce the outstanding mortgage. This means that you repay your mortgage sooner, and that you pay less overall in the long run.

If this sounds confusing, don't worry; it is an unusual way of looking at things, but it is a very useful one. The actual benefit to you is the same as if you had invested your £5,000 somewhere else that paid you the same rate of interest as that which is charged on your mortgage. And this gain is tax free to boot! Imagine getting five, six or seven per cent on your savings - without having to pay tax on this either!

These flexible mortgages have only recently become available. Why now? Well, Jan asks the same question... Such schemes have been available in South Africa for the past 15 years. Jan just mutters and speculates on the likely reasons, which may be resistance to change, reluctance to lose extra interest charges and antiquated mainframe computer systems that are incapable of handling such schemes. These are all likely reasons. Having been involved in Nedbank's introduction of similar flexible arrangements, when Jan first came to live in the UK, he was amazed (and aghast) to discover that nobody had heard of them here. Now they have, and jolly good schemes they are too – so use them!

Time scales

Both saving and borrowing can be divided into three time scales, which are short-term, medium term and long term.

Short-term savings are for those things that you are likely to need within a year, such as warm winter clothing, new bed linen, new curtains, vehicle tax and insurance or a holiday.

Medium-term savings are for periods of one to five years, such as replacing a vehicle, replacing a household appliance or household repairs and refurbishment.

Long-term savings refers to periods of over five years. For example: retirement and major additions or alterations to the home. It is possible to finance this by adding to your mortgage but this means that you will pay higher monthly installments and that you will be paying for this over a very long period of time. If possible, aim to clear your mortgage and to own your house sooner rather than later, so it may be worth looking into other forms of finance for this kind of thing.

What kind of savings scheme is best for you?

The answer to this depends upon how much disposable income you can spare; your attitude to savings, your short, medium and long-term goals and more. In this chapter we will look at a variety of savings methods that are suitable for ordinary people, and we will make some comments about the way these behave and the purposes that you might use them for. The message here though is always to save *something*, however small the amount, because you will need to have something behind you in the months and years to come.

Small savers

Long before we all became accustomed to using banks, many British people saved money in a National Savings

Ordinary Account at the Post Office. Reassuringly, the blue savings book looks much as it did more than fifty years ago. In theory, this is not suitable for large amounts of money as the rate of interest in this account has always been low, but at the moment it actually compares well with an instant access account at a bank. Even better, there is no income tax deducted on the first £70 interest that you make each year on this account or £140 if the account is in joint (two) names.

Children over the age of seven can use this account, and as the nice gentleman or lady at the post office writes down the sum that has been put in, children can see their money mounting up.

Our verdict

It is handy to be able to nip down to the local post office and plonk the odd tenner into this account. When it has accumulated, you should move it elsewhere if you can get a better rate of interest and still keep your money safe.

Premium bonds

In Britain, the premium bonds that we buy at the post office are a much older form of raffle than the national lottery but they are just as much fun. You will need to put in a minimum of £100 at first and then you can add batches of £10 at a time. You may win anything from £50 to one million pounds, and the winnings are tax-free. At the time of writing, the amount that you can put into Premium Bonds has recently been raised to £30,000 per person. Unless you invest up to this limit, your chances of winning a really big prize are pretty slim but there is always the chance of picking up the occasional fifty quid. Even if you never win anything, you can take your money back out at any time – and you can't do this with any other kind of lottery. Naturally, there is no interest at all on premium bonds, but in the present climate nothing is paying much interest, so the money that you put by in this way is keeping its value pretty well.

Our verdict

Premium bonds suit the person who has decent savings scheme elsewhere but who fancies putting a little away on the chance of an occasional windfall.

Other National Savings schemes

A visit to a main post office is well worth it. Pick up the many booklets that relate to National Savings and you will find a dazzling array of ideas. Whatever you want to put by and whatever your purpose you will find something that can accommodate you. The information in the booklets is easy to understand. If you have access to the Internet, punch up www.nationalsavings.co.uk and see what's on offer.

When stock markets are booming or and banks are offering high rates of interest, National Savings schemes are not attractive, but at the moment they compare surprisingly favourably with other methods of saving. As long as the country remains in one piece, your money will be safe. If you want to put money away for a set period of several years, don't take something with a fixed rate of interest, because when interest rates rise again, you will be stuck with a low one. National Savings even offer ISAs (see the chapter on investing).

Many schemes are for set periods of five years but these can be cashed in early if you need the money. You will lose some or all of the interest if you do this, but you can get your initial investment and often also some of the interest back in addition.

Our verdict

These savings schemes are safe, but most of them don't offer a high rate of interest, so normally one would look for something better but at the moment they compare well with other methods of saving. If you have a sizable amount of money to invest, you must spread your investment rather than sticking it all into one scheme.

What kind of savings?

Consider saving in the same light that you do with money that you borrow. For instance, are you looking at short, medium or long term savings? Do you want something that will pay you a regular income or something that you leave in place for a period of time and that pays some kind of bonus when you cash it in? Also consider your age. If you are young, you can cope with a certain amount of risk in exchange for a higher return, but if you are older you will look at safety first.

If you need an account that is instantly accessible, see that there is some real interest being paid on the one that you choose. Current accounts at banks do pay interest but it can be so low as to be invisible, especially if you go into overdraft. Some instant access savings schemes (deposit accounts, prime accounts, premium accounts) are not much better. Read the leaflets that different banks, building societies and even supermarkets put out and see who offers what for the amount of money that you wish to put by. Some accounts hold money for specific period of time, such as 30, 60, 90 or 365 days, and these pay a higher rate of interest. Some banks have telephone or postal accounts that offer a better rate; and some of the new Internet banks compare very favourably as well.

Whether you use Internet banking or not depends upon how happy you are to do things this way and whether you feel that you can trust these organisations to still be there in a few years' time. Some Internet banks are attached to normal banks while others seem to pop up out of nowhere. Consider whether you think that the institution will still be there five years down the line. We all know how difficult it is to get through on the phone or on the net when the lines are busy. This may be very useful to those who live in an area that is far from conventional banks, but do give it some thought before diving in to something this new. For example, we recently read an account in a newspaper about a lady whose pin number was accidentally reset by her Internet bank, and it took months before she could gain access to her money!

Supermarket banks are another strange idea, as is the Virgin organisation. It may seem odd to involve such a serious thing as your savings in firms that sell cabbages, CDs, airline seats or underwear, but if they work, then why not use them? Do bear in mind that all financial institutions brag about their services, but not all of them live up to expectations. Also, there is often small print that is very technical and which is designed to minimise some of the major drawbacks.

If you are likely to apply for a mortgage, you may wish to look at flexible and offset schemes that combine mortgages and savings or that offset the interest you make on your savings against the interest that you pay on your mortgage. These vary a lot in their scope, so you should look at a number of them. We will deal with these in more detail in the chapter on mortgages, but in general, it is preferable to keep things simple, so don't go for gimmicky or trendy products, stick to the more simple, straightforward things in life.

The main thing is to work out which type of account suits your needs and to shop around to see what interest rates are on offer. Even if you have been with a particular bank for donkey's years and you want to stay there, you can still open a savings account elsewhere. The only loyalty you need is the loyalty that you owe yourself.

The old-style bank manager no longer exists, so there is a tendency for some institutions to take the view that, as long as their lending is secure, it is the client's responsibility to look after his own interests. Banks, financial institutions, credit card companies, insurance companies and others try hard to entice you away from your current arrangements. Whether you sit tight or make changes, do ensure that you look after your own interests – just as they are doing with theirs.

Top tips

Buy newspapers for their money pages, as these will show you the best rates for different kinds of accounts at any particular time. Ceefax or the BBC business website (www.bbc.co.uk) also carry up to date information on all things financial free of charge. Go into every place that offers a saving scheme and make comparisons.

Calculation of interest

Depending upon the scheme you choose to use, interest may be calculated daily, monthly, quarterly or annually. The best schemes are those that calculate interest daily. Some flexible mortgage schemes that allow you to put extra money in and to take it out when you need it work this way. This can make a real difference to the amount of interest you gain over a period of time and also to the amount you pay on your mortgage.

Sasha thinks this comment about the way that interest is calculated could do with a few words of explanation. For example you already have £10 in the Ebenezer Scrooge Savings Company and you add another £10 to this each week for a year. By the end of the year you have put a further £520 in the account, but you would still only be accruing interest on the first tenner if the interest were calculated on an *annual* basis. Jan gets hot under the collar about this one, as he feels that anything more than monthly interest is a rip-off. A National Savings Ordinary Account calculates interest on an annual basis, but as this is usually used for very small savings it doesn't make much difference in the long run. When it comes to larger savings, opt for the most frequent calculation that you can find – among other considerations.

Simple and compound interest

Simple interest is the interest that is added once to an original sum. The words "per cent" roughly mean "for each hundred", so adding 10% interest to £100 means adding £10 to the original £100. (£100 + £10 = £110).

If we do the same sum for £1,000, it looks like this: £1,000 + £100 = £1,100.

Now if we were to add 10% *simple* interest each year for five years, the picture would look like this:

Start point: £1,000
After 1 year: £1,100
After 2 years: £1,200
After 3 years: £1,300
After 4 years: £1,400
After 5 years: £1,500

Compound interest means that not only the original investment but also the interest gathers interest, so the system works like this:

Start point: £1,000
After 1 year: £1,100
After 2 years: £1,210
After 3 years: £1,321
After 4 years: £1,432
After 5 years: £1,543

This is called *capitalism,* and no other political system works quite like it. At the moment, no investment will give you an interest rate of 10%, but you can see that any rate of interest can build up your money as long as you leave your original investment in place and add a little more to it on a regular basis.

Annuities

Annuities are schemes that are offered by insurance companies that sell pension schemes. You pay a set amount into the pension each month by direct debit until retirement age. At the end of the period, your money is invested into an annuity as a lump sum, and then you are paid a fixed amount annually or otherwise, depending upon the terms of the annuity. We will come back to this in more detail in the chapter on pensions. Take plenty of advice from a variety of sources before buying an annuity.

Tax tips

If you don't pay tax then you must ask the bank for form R85 and you will receive your interest gross (no tax deducted). If you forget to do this, you can ask the Inland Revenue to refund your tax. If you pay tax at a higher rate than the basic one, take a "tax paid" scheme and top this up by paying the extra tax at the end of the year. In most cases, it is up to you to advise the Inland Revenue of the interest you have earned. It is always best to be honest. The meagre bit of money that you would save by avoiding the tax is not worth the chance of being investigated and possibly prosecuted, and then having a black mark against your name in the Inland Revenue's record books.

Capital Gains Tax is a different animal. The two normal sources of capital gains are shares that go up in value and the rise in the price of a house or other property when you come to sell it. This doesn't apply to the house that you live in but it would apply to a second home. Selling a business or business arrangements also attract Capital Gains Tax.

Top tips

There are only two forms of saving that can keep ahead of inflation over the long term. One is in a mortgage that pays off a property and the second is the stock market - assuming that the stock market is doing well most of the time. Others may just about keep up or lag seriously behind.

APR - Annual Percentage Rate and AER - Annual Equivalent Rate

What a moveable feast these are! Does anyone really know what they mean? Those who set them, talk about them, sell them, use them or blind us with science may know what they mean by this, but what do these things really mean - and are they any use to us?

Jan is the first to say that Sasha has a very good grip on financial matters for someone who has not worked in the field, but Sasha says that as far as these two concepts are concerned, she is happy to hand over to Jan.

APR – Annual Percentage Rate

APR is used to simplify the comparison of different borrowing rates. It is worked out by converting different kinds of rates into what they would be if they were charged once a year, payable in arrears. All related charges, like up-front and administrative costs, are meant to be included, so if the APR is calculated properly, you can just compare one APR to the next and choose a suitable one. Unfortunately, some institutions have slightly different ideas of how to calculate APR, so comparisons are not always possible. Furthermore, you can't compare credit card rates with overdrafts or loans, because each works differently. You can compare one card's APR to another or one loan's APR to another.

My view is that the intention behind the creation of APRs is good, as it tries to help you to choose the best deal for your purpose. Any institution that tries to manipulate the standard APR calculation is not acting in your interests – whatever their reasoning. There are websites that do comparisons on these for you and they sometimes pick up these differences and point them out. It is worth noting such points because the institutions may try to overcharge in other ways as well.

AER – Annual Equivalent Rate

The AER does the same as the APR, except that it is used for savings and investments where you earn interest as opposed to where you pay it. The calculation is different but it converts different rates into what they would be if the interest was compounded and paid annually. Once again, any related charges are meant to be included, except for tax, which in practice, is often deducted at source.

Although neither APR nor AER are completely accurate, they do give you a relatively useful tool when you are trying to compare different deals. What would be very useful would be for the authorities to simplify the tax-efficient options that are available to us all. For instance, the ISA concept is far too complicated to be an incentive for the average person to grasp. There are just too many rules, conditions, limitations and considerations involved. We really need a much simpler way of saving our money, especially when one considers that the country needs to encourage saving rather than encouraging people to spend up and beyond their limits.

Back to Sasha

Did you understand all that? I admit that I am struggling with it. I think it means that the APR is a way of comparing means of *borrowing* money - as long as you are comparing like to like (one credit card with another or one loan to another etc.) The AER is a way of comparing methods of *saving* money. This kind of stuff is worked out by clever people who may try to juggle the figures to show themselves in a good light and while it seems to be good, I still prefer to work out for myself just how many beans make five.

5

Borrowing Money

Let us all be happy within our means, even if we have to
borrer money to do it with.
Artemus Ward.
Be not made a beggar by banqueting on borrowing.
Ecclesiasticus.

We all have to borrow from time to time if only in the form
of a mortgage, but when things are up in the air, it is better
to confine borrowing to absolute necessities. The trick here
is to consider the difference between needing and wanting.
Your central heating may pack up, the car that gets you to
work may give up the ghost, the washing machine may sink
into a puddle of suds or some other disaster may occur. In
these cases you may need to borrow money.

Now consider the words in this recent brochure from a
high street bank.

"We understand that you may need to borrow money for
a whole host of reasons. It could be that holiday that you

never thought you could afford. The dream wedding and even dreamier honeymoon. Tropical birds, tropical fish. Cars or caravans or conservatories. Even the mounting cost of higher education."

Look at the things that the brochure suggests warrant taking out a loan. Sure, higher education may be important and a nice wedding could be classed as vital, although the honeymoon could be deferred for a while if necessary. But *tropical birds and fish!* It was the word *need* in the brochure that astonished us. Do us a favour! The logic behind suggesting that you should go into debt to buy a parrot or a tank of guppies is based on the greed of an organisation that just wants another poor sod paying them interest!

The following are all very nice to have - but are they necessities?

~ A conservatory.
~ A caravan.
~ A new car simply because you feel like upgrading.
~ A computer to play games on.
~ An exotic holiday.
~ An expensive party.
~ A pet that is expensive to buy, feed, care for and insure.

These things can wait until you can buy them without having to borrow. It is good to have nice things and it is right to have goals, so start to save for what you want. If you really need a holiday, at least save up three quarters of what it will cost and then borrow some top up money, but don't even do this if your job or your future is uncertain.

On the other hand...

Having said all the foregoing, Pierce Brosnan was invited to go to Hollywood to discuss making a film. He and his wife didn't have the money for the trip, so they took a bank loan for a central heating system. The couple used the loan money to go to Hollywood where Pierce made a few movies and then landed the James Bond job. Now he could probably buy central heating systems for everyone in Britain.

A few years ago, a friend of ours wanted to get out of the renting trap and take a mortgage. Being a first time buyer and self-employed into the bargain, this was not easy. One bank agreed to give him a mortgage if he could put down a 15% deposit on the property. He obtained a bank loan for the deposit and moved in. The property has since doubled in value and his bank loan is on the point of being fully paid off. Jan wouldn't advise anybody to go to Hollywood on spec or to buy a house that you can't afford, but Sasha says that sometimes you just have to follow your nose on these things.

Our verdict

There are times when it is worth taking a risk and taking a loan but it should be a *calculated* risk. Having said this, property is fetching top money right now and it will fall back in price, so this may not be the best time to take risks.

Borrowing in more detail

In the context of this chapter, the word *finance* means money that you borrow. There are almost as many ways of borrowing money as there are saving, but these mainly fall into three categories, which are short, medium and long term finance.

Short-term finance

This is money that you borrow for days, weeks or months. In theory, this could be a loan from a loved one to tide you over a difficult patch, an outstanding balance on a credit card, a very short-term loan (for no longer than a year) and an overdraft that you repay within a year.

Medium-term finance

This is money that you borrow for a period of one to five years, or in some cases a little longer. This usually means a bank or other loan, hire purchase, lease hire, a loan from a vehicle dealer, buying furniture on terms from a dealer and similar arrangements.

Long-term finance

This usually involves periods in excess of five years and typically, it may relate to a mortgage or perhaps re-mortgaging a property in order to extend or improve it.

Top tip

Never borrow long-term for medium-term purposes and never borrow medium-term for short-term purposes. Never increase your mortgage to pay for a luxury holiday. Imagine how you will feel fifteen years down the line knowing that you have a several more years of repayments to make for something that you can't even remember doing. Don't confuse *wanting* and *needing*.

Short-term finance - overdrafts

Here is one of the most misunderstood animals in the world of money (says Jan with a sigh). The average person approaches a bank for an overdraft when his car needs a service, when the washing machine blows up, when he wants a holiday or when something unexpected occurs. This is not the right purpose of an overdraft, but the bank staff may not actually know the right purpose, so how can they advise a customer of this?

An overdraft facility is intended for *short-term bridging finance* against the *definite* receipt of funds at a definite point in the near future. The timing of this should be absolutely beyond doubt. For instance, your annual bonus is not guaranteed until it is in your hot little hands. Such potentials as a hot tip on the horses, commission and so on are not definite. One thing that is definite is that interest will be charged on your overdraft.

Sure, we all get caught short at times, so an overdraft may be necessary in an emergency, but you must be confident that you can repay it from your normal income. An overdraft can never be a source of funds. You should try to put some money by for unforeseen circumstances. We know that we can't all do that, and we ourselves have sometimes been in the same boat, but before we run to the bank, we sit down and work out the difference between our needs and our wants, and we usually come to the conclusion that we can manage without buying whatever it was that we fancied.

Overdrafts are difficult to pay off, and when combined with bank loans, credit card balances and other debts, the interest that you pay racks up until you find yourself in a jam.

Those who work in banks have sales targets to meet, so they usually are happy to supply you with finance that they can earn interest on, provided the facility can be made safe enough from the bank's point of view. You may be delighted with your bank for allowing you to have an overdraft, but you must judge whether this is safe enough from your point of view. Also remember that an overdraft can be called up overnight. This means that the bank may insist on the overdraft being paid off in full - and this is guaranteed to happen at the worst possible moment.

It is worth checking the interest rate on an overdraft against that on your credit card, because the card might actually be a cheaper option for short-term finance. At the very least, while you continue to make the minimum payments on your card, it won't be called up, while an overdraft can be called up overnight if the bank deems it to be necessary.

Top tips

As long as you keep the words, *short-term*, *bridging*, *definite* and *near future* in mind, you won't go far wrong. If something goes radically wrong in your financial life, talk to the bank rather than simply ignoring letters. At worst, make an offer to repay a debt at a small monthly rate. This will be acceptable as long as the interest is covered and if it is reasonable for your circumstances.

Never try to start a business by means of an overdraft. This just doesn't work and invariably you will suffer. You may talk the bank into giving you an overdraft by tricking them as to its purpose or by giving them your home as security but it doesn't mean that you are doing yourself any favours. From years of lending for all kinds of purposes, the banks know very well what lending is sensible and what is likely to become a bad debt.

Our verdict

It's wise to have an overdraft facility in place, especially if you don't keep much money in your current account and if you have direct debits, because one bit of overspending can leave you overdrawn on your account. An *unauthorised* overdraft is expensive but if you dip into a facility that is already allowed for you can live with the results. Try to keep a minimum of £100 in your current account and you won't need to use your facility at all.

Short-term finance - credit cards

We cover these in detail in the chapter on cards, but here are more ideas that link with this kind of short-term finance. If you only repay the minimum amount on your card each month you will soon find the debt growing out of control. Interest rates on cards are normally higher than they are for a bank loan.

If you are struggling to pay off your cards, *do* something about this. Avoid buying new things, take on extra work and ask your spouse or another family member to do the same. Consider selling something. Boot sales are great fun and they are also a wonderful way of clearing clutter from your home while making some extra money. If you have debts, you can use this money to pay them off; otherwise this is a great source of finance for meals out or for a holiday.

Even those of you who hate maths will understand the following equation:

Four boot sales = one cheapy holiday in the sun.

For those whose minds are more attuned to verbal quizzes than to maths, try this one for size:

Gather as many credit cards as are offered to you and borrow money on every one of them. Add a dose of debt from a mortgage, bank loan, overdraft, hire purchase payments and then work out whether you can expect more sympathy from these financial institutions or from your garden gnome?

Medium term finance - bank or other loans

All decent people live beyond their incomes nowadays, and those who aren't respectable live beyond other people's.
Anonymous 19th century wit.

Loans can be very useful, but you must avoid becoming loaded down with them or committing all your spare cash from your wages. Try not to take more than one medium-term loan per family, and only take this out for concrete goods that are absolutely necessary. It is easy to convince ourselves that we deserve treats, but in reality we only deserve them if we have earned or saved the money for them. Having said all this, interest rates on loans are low at the moment, but if you take a loan do ensure that the rate of interest on the loan is fixed for the entire period of the loan. If it is index linked to the Bank of England base rate, the interest on the loan will rise if the base rate rises.

Nowadays we are bombarded by advertising for loans at very reasonable rates. Some only offer low rates if you borrow a large sum of money, others are fairly generous even for smaller sums. Read the small print on the leaflets and check the rates for he amount that you need to borrow and ensure that the rate is fixed for the entire period of the loan.

It may be worth taking out a loan in order to consolidate your other debts. The longer the period of the loan, the more interest you will pay overall although your monthly payments will be easier to cope with. Once you have consolidated your debts, don't run up any more of them.

Before leaving the subject of bank loans in particular, we recently heard a story about a couple of people aged around 60 who were told that they were ineligible for a loan because they were too old! We realise that the bank will look at a person's ability to repay a loan based on whether they have a job, own a property or on any other assets that they may have, but this does seem rather hard on a couple who could conceivably take some kind of work in order to repay a small loan.

Top tips

~   The best time to get a bank loan is now, as long as you get one with the interest rate fixed for the duration of the loan.

~   Don't limit yourself to banks, because the supermarkets, Automobile Association and other organisations have some good offers. At the time of writing, the Co-operative bank seems to have a good deal.

~ Don't go to some unknown outfit that advertises in the paper and elsewhere without checking the interest rates and the small print and also checking out their reputation.
~ Don't apply for several loans at the same time, as this alerts the credit checking companies that you have a problem. Defaulting on repayments earns you black marks on your credit records.
~ Use your loan for its original purpose rather than spending the money on something else.

Medium-term finance - students

A more worrying and very modern debt is the kind that students get into during their years of study. The theory is that once a student has his degree, he will get a well-paid job and quickly pay the loan back. But, what if the student drops out after a couple of years? And, what if he fails to achieve a degree? Even if he does, he has to start his working life with huge debts. In the current housing market, this means that even if he (or she) can get a mortgage, he will be strapped for cash for years and it will be very hard for him to buy a home or get married and start a family. We don't have an answer to this one. If a Labour government is not willing to support students with grants, then would a conservative one? The country needs trained and educated people, but the thought of incurring vast debts is bound to put many able young people off higher education, and this will be a loss to the nation's future.

Investigate the interest free loans that some financial organisations offer to students. These firms know that once someone has an account with their organisation, the chances are that they will remain with them for many years to come, so this is a good way for them to build their customer base.

Student credit cards do not offer advantageous rates, indeed a cash advance on such a card from one high street bank is currently running at 28%! No youngster should have to deal with such extortionate greed.

Top tips

~ If you think your own children might go to university, start to save for this as early as you can.
~ If you and your children get on well together, consider suggesting that they look for a course that is close to home so that they can continue to live at home.

Long-term finance - mortgages

A home is the largest investment that most of us will make in our lifetime. A home of your own is a safe refuge and a place where you can relax and enjoy your private life. It may be a place where you express your creativity in home-making or by making a garden. Once you have repaid the mortgage, it is yours and it is safe. You may move home from time to time, but the sentiment remains the same.

Never take chances with this important element of your life and never take your home for granted. Pay the mortgage off rather than borrowing money against it for luxuries such as a fancy car or timeshare. A common problem occurs when people put their home up as security for a business. Sure, the problem may be sorted out within a year or so – but what if it isn't? Cars, boats and caravans can crash or be stolen, timeshares are notorious for problems and a business that is in need of a large loan is not in good shape, especially a new business.

Another doubtful concept often offered to retired people is *equity release*. This means selling part of the house to a finance company in exchange for a lump sum. One of the drawbacks is that the property will very likely have to be sold when you die, to repay the loan. There can be some sense in this if you are living in dire poverty, but it should be avoided if at all possible. We don't advocate hanging onto something that you can't afford for no other reason than to pass it on to your children, but we do advise you to think hard about all the implications before going in for this idea. There are other, better options available.

Top tips

If you need something basic like an indoor bathroom, loft insulation or central heating, there may be local government grants that will go some way towards paying for this as part of a local energy saving plan. This may even apply if you need to replace an old central heating system (e.g. if it is over twelve years old).

Before you spend too much on home improvements, consider whether you want to live in the home for many years to come or to sell it and move on, as there is no point in paying top dollar for improvements that you are not going to enjoy in the long term. Consider whether the improvements that you make will price the house out of the area.

Our verdict

Never use your house as a means of finance for anything other than *itself*. Take a second mortgage for a loft conversion or an extension if you need this, as it will add value to the house, but that's all. Pay it off as quickly as you can.

We can't stress this point too strongly - the following is a quick, last-minute, pre-print insert. We have just read in the finance section of a respectable national newspaper, discussion of the pros and cons of taking a second mortgage to invest in the stock market. Sadly, the articles end up with the view that there might be risks, but that the possible income levels against a fixed, low-rate 5-year mortgage make this tactic reasonably worthwhile.

This is a very short-sighted viewpoint for short-term and volatile purposes like dabbling in the stock market. No one can yet guarantee that the doldrums are over and the markets are genuinely on the way up again. We still have a real possibility that somewhere in the world, something will trigger a global crisis, because, globally, reserves and resources are at a very low point. Thirdly, if things do get really bad, then *everything* gets bad, and you may easily be forced to sell investments at dismally low prices.

At present, uncertainty still rules, ok?

Worse still would be the idea of taking out an *overdraft* for dabbling in the market - the reason for this is that an overdraft can be called up overnight, for any reason, and this tends to happen at the worst possible moment. At least a mortgage doesn't have that drawback.

6

How Elastic is your Plastic?

He that hath lost his credit is dead to the world
G. Herbert. Outlandish Proverbs, AD 1640
A credit limit on a credit card is not real money, it is
virtual money, it is money creation. Unfortunately, some
people think they can spend this virtual money, virtually
without ever having to pay for it!
Jan Budkowski

Credit cards

Credit cards would not have taken off in the way that they have if they were not so very convenient. We can travel almost anywhere in the world without having to search for a bank in a foreign country so that we can change travellers cheques, and we can even make purchases over the Internet. The first cards were *charge cards,* which were convenient for travellers, but the balances had to be paid in full at the end of each month.

The trap that credit cards can set us is the element of *credit* that is involved in them. The outstanding balances on credit cards have now become so stratospheric that they may one day be responsible for devaluing the currency in some countries. There are currently 1,500 different cards available worldwide and hundreds of different arrangements. Conditions change within each system, so it is hard for us to keep up with what's going on.

How do you pay your balances?

In full each month
Here, the interest that the card charges is irrelevant. You might benefit from loyalty points or reduced price purchases, and some cards offer a cash-back arrangement. This is particularly useful for business people who use cards a lot. Don't save loyalty points for too long without using them up because the card company may suddenly decide to scrap or change the scheme. One company that offered air miles, most of which were one-way tickets to somewhere that nobody wanted to visit, but some offered long haul tickets that were worthwhile. However, by the time people came close to the number of points that they would need to take the trip, the air miles suddenly transformed themselves from a ticket to Sydney to a month's groceries! The moral here is to use them or lose them.

Most of the time
If you only spread the debt for a month or two at Christmas or for holidays the interest rate is not so vital. Bear in mind

that some card companies charge a hefty penalty for a late payment, so you must watch this when going on holiday.

You rarely clear them
For you, the interest rate is vital, while offers such as bargain flights are of little or no importance.

Using cards to obtain cash

Drawing cash from a bank or a cashpoint is expensive because the interest is higher than it is for goods bought on the card and there is an added handling fee. Keep this facility for emergencies or for holidays. If you read the small print on the sales forms you will see that in some cases cash advances that are protected by debt insurance carry an interest rate of 29%. Those who use these cards to draw cash on a regular basis would soon be up to their necks in unnecessary debt. Don't fall for the spiel that you see in junk mail for credit cards. Read the small print to see what is really going on behind the smokescreen.

Changing card companies

To change or not to change… ah, that is the story!

If you do not pay the balance off in full each month, and if the card that you have used for the past umpteen years has a high interest rate, it is worth applying for a different one. There is no need to chuck your old card away unless you are racking up debts, in which case your best bet is to choose one card company that offers a lower interest rate, and then slice up all your other cards and toss them away.

One benefit of keeping the old card is that your credit limit will have increased year on year, so this gives you a fallback position against possible future problems. However, if you are financially undisciplined, or if your lifestyle means that your expenditure is regularly running at too high a rate for your income, this can be too tempting. A line of credit is not free money – it is an invitation to free debt! You can bet that nobody asks you whether you are being tempted beyond your power of resistance. The card company is interested in what is safe for *them,* not what might be safe for you.

Balance transfers

If you have a lingering debt, applying for some other card and taking advantage of a low interest or even an interest free six month holiday is tempting and many people do move their debt around until (hopefully) they are able to clear it for good. However, there are some hidden traps to take into consideration.

The card that you move to may charge you an administration or handling fee for moving your debt to them. This is barely understandable if you open a new card because they want your debt and they shouldn't charge you for giving it to them.

If you move your balance from one card company to another that you already deal with, a fee is a complete rip-off, because all the company needs to do is to ask a clerk to make a few clicks on a computer. The company is not setting up a new card and they aren't losing your business. In such a case, work out whether the interest you are likely to pay is more, less or much the same as the handling fee before you make the change. Check the terms and conditions and try phoning the card company and complaining about this, because such companies do sometimes back down and waive such fees if you "phone and moan" about it.

If you move your balance and then make more purchases on the card that you have moved the debt to, the money that you pay the card company may be taken from the interest free balance transfer before it comes off whatever purchases you have been making. This could have the effect of costing you more in interest payments in the long run!

You can phone and moan about this issue too, and the chances are that the credit card company will agree to put your repayments against that part of the debt that has not resulted from a balance transfer. Few people think of doing this, so the card companies rely on your ignorance or your lack of willingness to phone them and to take them on in this way. Worse still, some companies now only allow a six month interest free period if you continue to top up the debt by making more purchases on the card! Once again, read the small print and check the terms and conditions. If the company doesn't make them clear even in their small print, then phone and moan. Don't trust them and don't leave them any loopholes – they don't leave you any, do they?

If you apply for a number of new cards in order to take advantage of interest free periods, remember that every time you apply for a card the information goes into a credit record database. Down the line, some other type of lender might assume that you have problems with money and thus be reluctant to lend in future.

Credit card companies and banks have sliding scales for the interest that they charge each client, so the worse you are at clearing debts, the more interest they charge.

Top tips

~ Pay off overdrafts as soon as you can, then clear or at least reduce credit card debts as soon as you can.

~ If you have a high credit limit, ignore it and set your own lower limit.

~ If you know that you have a particular danger area, take cash with you and leave your cards and chequebook at home. Sasha and her daughter, Helen, dare not take credit cards or cheque books anywhere near their local garden centres...

~ Why not buy Christmas presents throughout the year when such items are less expensive than they are in December. Buy Christmas cards, paper, crackers, baubles, tinsel and even a plastic tree immediately after Christmas and put the stuff away for the following year.

~ If your family spends a fortune at Christmas, don't try to keep up with them; this is not a time to keep up with the Jones's. Tell your loved ones that you love them very much but that your presents and entertaining will be modest. A limit of £5 to £10 per gift should be plenty and they should understand and respect you for this. We all want to give our children nice things at Christmas but we shouldn't turn them into tyrants who bully us into spending what we can't afford. Be honest and tell them what money you have available for them and ask them to choose one thing that they really want and to be satisfied with that. Perhaps point out that love is a two-way thing and that you do love them but that they must demonstrate their love for you by looking after you as well. They won't have thought of that, but when you point out that love means thinking of others as well as oneself, they will get the message. Whatever religion you belong to, Christmas is not about breaking the bank, it is about giving thanks and showing love.

When you have overdone things

Money, it turned out, is exactly like sex. You thought of little else if you didn't have it, and other things if you did.
James Baldwin.

If you have a credit card debt, you can take a variety of actions that depend upon your circumstances. Here is a nice story:

Kay and Mike met and fell in love. They knew that their extremely difficult previous partners would fight them as far as money and goods were concerned, so they decided not to give themselves added pressure by fighting over goods that they had once owned. They rented a flat and started again, more or less from scratch. For a while they had no choice but to use their credit cards and this landed them with a debt. Once they had what they absolutely needed, they cut up their cards. Kay phoned the credit card company and told them about the situation, after which they agreed to pay off the debt at a set rate each month. Once the debt was cleared, they applied for new credit cards, which they kept purely for emergencies. This was a clever use of the only source of finance that Kay and Mike could turn to during this difficult time and it showed clever money management on their part.

If you are in debt and you have several cards. cancel all but one of them, along with a supplementary card for your partner if appropriate. If necessary, arrange a bank loan and use it to clear debts, because you will then have no option but to pay the loan off each month until it is cleared. If you take a loan for the purpose of clearing credit card debts, cut up your credit cards and don't apply for any more until the loan is cleared.

Business credit cards

Businesses can use cards and they can even dish them out to their staff. Some business cards charge very high rates of interest, so think twice before using these.

Which card should you opt for?

There is no quick answer, but if you are thinking of getting a credit card or of switching from one to another, check the newspapers and the Internet for the best deals.

Direct debit payments

When Jan first settled in Britain he was astonished to discover that we couldn't settle our credit card bill by direct debit, especially in view of the fact that the South African bank that he had worked in had accepted direct debit payments as long ago as 1981. The computer systems for this are expensive, so older institutions are less likely to change what they already have in order to accommodate this method. Some newer companies will happily take a minimum payment on direct debit. This is a good idea because you can keep out of trouble by paying something even when you are on holiday, thus avoiding late payment penalties.

Change of address

If you move house, it is *essential* to inform the card companies of your new address immediately.

A friend of ours got into an unbelievable mess due to this. He had a charge card and a credit card with the same company, but while he informed the credit card arm of this company that he had moved but he forgot to tell the charge card arm. Naturally, the two departments of the same company didn't connect, so one didn't automatically inform the other of his change of address.

He rarely used the charge card, but for some reason during the rush and hurry of moving house, he had spent £48 on his charge card and this had slipped his mind. The company sent letters to his previous address, but these didn't reach him. The penalties for late payment started to rack up until they far exceeded the small sum that had originally been owed. If a person rather than a computer system had looked at this, they would have realised that this was some kind of error, but in the event, he ended up being reported to one of those debt listing businesses – Experian, Equifax or Equally Awful and all for a £48 debt! After three months of argy-bargy, he got his name taken off these debt companies and he even got the late payment fees waived. Part of the problem was the difficulty in getting to speak to a human being! The so-called telephone help lines seem to be put in place to distance the organisation from its clients.

Debit cards

Debit cards take money directly from your current account, so you are less likely to overspend, as they feel more like real money. There is no interest charged on these and you can't overdraw because they won't work when there is no money left in the kitty.

Please bear in mind that there can be a stiff handling charge when you stick a debit card in some cashpoints, especially the non-bank ones that you sometimes see in corner shops. This is great for an emergency, but not as a regular means of obtaining cash. Here is another area where some banks overcharge. The actual cost of processing a withdrawal is less than 40p, whereas you may be charged £1 or more. Watch your use of this system!

Fraud

Identity fraud is the fastest growing crime in the UK and there is no reason to think that it doesn't exist in other, less well-regulated countries. This kind of thing flourishes in crime-ridden South Africa. With a combination of a bank account number, name and address, a confidence trickster can get all the documents needed in order to create a new identity. In point of fact, this will be *your* identity, and you could suddenly find yourself technically the proud owner of a couple of dozen credit cards. The thief can draw money or spend up to the limit on those cards, leaving you to pick up the bills. A thief can obtain this information from the Internet, but an easier way is to go through your garbage, or even presumably through garbage bags at a dump. Once he has a gas bill with your address on it, plus a bank statement, credit card slips or any other official information, he can build his new identity, move house and do anything he likes – at your expense.

Invest in a shredder, ensure that it is the kind that cuts the paper into crosscut pieces and use it for anything that has any of your details on it. When travelling in dodgy places, it may actually be worth reverting to the old method of buying traveller's cheques and cashing them at a local bank. Only buy from reputable Internet organisations (such as Amazon for books) and don't leave documents lying around in hotels or strange places.

Take care when using a cashpoint. Ensure that nobody can see the pin number that you have to punch in. In South Africa, crooks set up video cameras in buildings over the street from cash points, and in that way they can see the pin numbers being punched in. Then it is an easy job to mug the person and steal the cards. Armed with the cards and the pin numbers, they could clear the accounts, leaving the poor victim to pay the debt. If a card gets stuck in a cashpoint or if the cashpoint doesn't work properly, it could be because something has been put into it that will record your number. If anything happens that you are not happy with, phone the card company immediately and they will void the card so that nobody can use it. Very importantly, never write your pin number down and never ever keep it with your card.

Top tips

~ If you have several cards, you can change the pin numbers on all of them to one number so that you only have one number to remember. Don't make this number anything obvious such as your date of birth, just dream up something vague and meaningless to anyone else and keep to it. It must be very meaningless and difficult to hit on; if it isn't remember that the thief then has the code to all your cards!

~ Take the credit or debit card's phone number with you when travelling and ensure that you can get at it even if your bags have been stolen.

~ Wear a body belt and keep important numbers, addresses, cards and other details in that. You can still take a handbag or shopping bag for all your other bits and pieces but don't leave sensitive stuff lying around in it.

~ Handbags are often not as secure as you would like to believe; even if the strap(s) are really well sewn into the bag - and most aren't - a bag can be snatched off your shoulder in no time at all, often leaving your arm scratched and hurt. It is best to have a long strap that goes over your head as well. Keep the opening flap turned in to your body, and preferably have zips on all the openings.

Card protection insurance

Your card company or your bank will try to sell you this insurance. It is a good idea to take this out, but bear in mind that some companies offer this service free with their cards. If yours does not, then point this out and ask if you can have the protection free of charge – they may agree, and if they don't, then consider changing your card supplier, unless the charge is nominal.

Store cards

Some stores offered payment schemes years before the credit card era. Store cards may offer a ten per cent discount on a purchase when you sign up with them, and some continue to offer occasional discounts or incentives from time to time as you go along. The idea is that you select the goods that you want and pay them off over time.

The interest that these cards charge is often very high - certainly much higher than any ten per cent discount that is offered and it is often much higher than other forms of borrowing. The news this past week has been about a Treasury Select Committee report that found one store card charging interest at 32.5%, and others also charging not much less. With the Bank of England base rate at 3.5% at the moment - the lowest in nearly 50 years - the Committee's conclusion was that these rates were "fleecing" customers. One of the major credit card companies was also found to be charging nearly 25%, and thus in the same league as some of the store cards. When you consider that some more socially responsible store cards are charging only 13%, it is clear that you really have to be very careful as to which card you choose They can be a terrible trap for the unwary, so unless you have pots of money and don't care what you pay for your clothes, leave these extortionate cards alone. One last tip: if the card's *full* terms and conditions and interest rates are not readily available for you to take away and read *before* you sign up, then don't sign up! This has been a major complaint in the past, and should no longer be happening with any ethical organisation.

Loyalty cards

Supermarkets, garages, shops and many other organisations offer loyalty cards. These are not credit cards, they just tot up what you have spent and allocate points that you can exchange for something. Take them all, they cost nothing and you may get something out of them from time to time, but shop where you want to rather than where *they* want you to. The only type of loyalty card that is worth having is the one that allows you to get something off your shopping bill. One supermarket sends their loyalty customers coupons. The coupons rarely match what you want to buy and even if they do, it is a huge pain in the neck to have to look around the supermarket in order to save a few shillings. Even if you have the patience for this, you can bet that some early bird customer has got there before you and snapped up the bargain!

Two of our local supermarkets offer a reduction in the price of petrol if we spend over a certain amount of money with them and as long as we buy the fuel within a few days of doing the shopping. This benefits both parties and it is immediate, so we don't lose out by hanging onto some card and losing the benefit later on when they company decides to scrap or change the system.

Top tips

If you apply for a card and are refused, you can appeal to the card company. Supply evidence to support your claim. Check the credit listing companies (Experian and Equifax) in case you have a black mark against your name, as this can sometimes happen by mistake. You can easily do a search for a small fee, currently £2.

7

Debt – Mortgaging your Future

Creditors have better memories than debtors
J Howell. Proverbs, AD 1659
Excessive use of credit is cited as a major cause of non-
business bankruptcy, second only to unemployment.
An anonymous financial guru

Debt in itself is not a problem. We all have debts of one kind or another at some time or another – the most common being a mortgage on our homes.

Other forms of debt are perfectly valid, *as long as they are used correctly for their intended purpose.* Here are some examples of what we mean:

A common long-term debt

A mortgage is used to finance the purchase of your home. This is a long-term debt and the objective is to repay the mortgage and then own the property fully at the end of the mortgage period. You don't want to be saddled later in life by mortgage payments that you have to find from your pension. Perhaps, when you eventually pass away, this would mean that your children could inherit the property, thereby getting rid of their own mortgages and having a better life than you did.

The objective should always be to pay the mortgage off as soon as possible and never to raise a further mortgage for some frivolous purpose such as a fancy car, a special holiday or some other matter that is unrelated to the property itself. It can make sense to increase a mortgage later to enlarge or improve your home, as this may be a cheaper and less inconvenient option than moving house, but this is *all* that you should ever use the security of your property for.

Statistics show that most people move house on average every seven years, and take out a new mortgage each time. The chances are that each mortgage is larger than the previous one, so you need to consider whether you can guarantee having a higher salary or keeping your job down the line, to finance the higher repayments. Our best advice is to get your mortgage repaid as soon as you can and then leave the equity where it is – in your bricks and mortar!

Some thoughts on debt

When you go into debt you are spending money that you hope to earn in the future. This is pretty much bound to happen sometimes - perhaps when moving house or if you give up work in order to start a family. This is fair enough if you know that your job is secure. In other cases, it is seriously depressing, because when you fancy buying something, you won't be able to. Spending what you think will come in from your normal income is bad enough, but spending on the basis of an expected rise or bonus is best avoided. If this doesn't come or if your job falls apart, you will be lumbered with an existing debt before others start to pile in.

Consider the difference between *wanting* and *needing*, because when uncertain times come along, you should only buy what you *need*. Also consider that old saying, "watch the pennies and let the pounds take care of themselves". This is because it is often the little things that eat away at your available funds. Things always go wrong at just the wrong moment, so you must keep something behind you for unexpected expenses.

The most common form of debt is caused by overspending on credit cards. It is hard not to do this, and we all do it from time to time. Nobody can keep a running total in his head of what has already gone out on the card , and a card doesn't feel the same as does a diminishing pile of cash in one's wallet. Store cards are real traps, so don't fall for the offer of a 10% discount if you take up a store card. Sure, the girl in the shop will look at you as though you are crazy for turning down her nice offer, but remember that she and her friends in the shop may be on a commission for all the cards they can offload on the vast army of innocents out there.

It may well be an idea to work out what you can afford and to set up a weekly budget. This is easier to cope with than a monthly one. Then put a week's money in your wallet or purse and leave the credit cards at home.

When things go wrong

The main thing is not to hide your head in the sand because even one missed payment on your mortgage can give you a bad credit record and it could put your home at risk. The same goes for rent arrears. One missed Council Tax payment can land you in court. This book is not aimed at business people, but if you are in business, you must pay your VAT because non-payment of VAT can also land you in court. Tell these organisations that you have a problem, as they may allow you to pay interest only, or you may be able to *re-schedule* your debt, thus paying it off at a lower rate over a longer period of time.

Make a list and put the items under headings of priority and non-priority debts. The most important of these is council tax, because if that is not paid, you will eventually end up in prison. Then pay your mortgage, income tax, rent and if applicable, VAT. Then take the smallest debt or the credit card with the smallest amount owing on it and pay this off as quickly as you can. You may wonder why we advise tackling the smallest amount first, but there is a good psychological reason for it. Once you have paid the thing off, you will feel as though you are getting somewhere and that gives you the incentive to tackle the next one on the list.

If you have a high interest card, move this balance to a card that allows you to shift a balance for six months at a zero rate of interest, but do check to see if there is an admin charge that may be higher than the potential benefit. Then you can gradually nibble away at all your other debts until you are free of all the millstones that are hanging around your neck.

Consolidation

Much is made of taking one loan to consolidate a variety of debts. This can be useful, but watch what you are doing here. The newspapers and junk mail are full of offers for this, but some have high rates of interest, high service charges or some other hidden piece of unpleasantness. A bank loan is the best for this, but then you must cut up your credit cards and stop spending anything above what is absolutely necessary for a while.

Look for an unsecured loan and think twice before taking out repayment protection cover on the loan, because this is expensive and it often only pays out under certain very limited circumstances, such as if you die. Payment protection is a form of insurance that is also often a way for the lending company to make money at your expense, so avoid such pitfalls.

Ensure that there is no early payment redemption fee, in case you discover that you can clear the loan earlier than you thought you could. Also check that the loan interest rate is fixed. That means that the amount of interest is settled when you agree the loan and that it will not shoot up if the base rate or anything else starts to climb.

Consolidation loans that are advertised on the television, in newspapers and on leaflets that drop through your door may have a very high rate of interest, and they are always *secured* loans, which can put your home in peril.

Some of these companies are quick to call up their security at the first sign of a default, so take care with your repayments.

It is worth noting that a recent court case has brought to light that many of these agreements are not watertight; for example, if a payment protection policy was made compulsory but was not included as a cost of the loan, and clearly shown, the loan may be unenforceable, saving you from unjust legal action and repayments. If your lender asks you to sign a fresh or amended agreement, for any reason at all, don't sign in haste - that would be a most unusual kind of request, and is likely not to be in your interests. Check it out with a solicitor or the Citizen's Advice Bureau first.

There are probably thousands of such flawed loan agreements around and it is worth your while to check out the wording of your current agreement. Do this through a solicitor, as there are some very technical issues involved, and that is the only way to be certain.

What if you can't pay?

There is nothing that drives creditors batty faster than not knowing what is going on. Remember the story of our friend who owned £48 to a card company but wasn't aware of it? Because he was unaware of the debt, he did nothing about it, and that landed him in hot water.

All professional lenders know that if they bankrupt you they will get little or nothing back, so they are bound to listen if you talk to them about your problem. It may be that you lose your job or that some other unexpected problem arises. Under such circumstances, you may be able to pay a trickle off your debts until you are able to earn money again and start to pay more.

Here is a true story. A friend called Peter was landed with a large accountant's bill which he couldn't pay. Peter phoned the accountant and offered to pay off £50 each month until it was cleared. The accountant was happy to allow him to do this and he didn't even charge Peter any interest for what was essentially a loan of several hundred pounds.

When all else fails

Let us never negotiate out of fear. But, let us never fear to negotiate.

John Fitzgerald Kennedy, on his inaugural address on the 20th of January 1961.

If you really don't know what to do, contact your local branch of the Citizens Advice Bureau (CAB) or find their details by ringing 020 7833 2181 or look them up on the Internet. They will put you in touch with a charitable organisation called The Consumer Credit Counselling Service (CCCS). You can also ring the CCCS on 0800 138 1111. They will help you to sort out your problems. This charity will take some of the misery from your shoulders by writing to your creditors. Be careful about consulting a private, professional credit-counselling firm, as there have been cases where some of them charge you a hefty fee or take a huge commission from every payment that you make. This can only add to your debt misery. Sasha's first husband once had a dreadful business setback and in desperation, he consulted one of these firms. They did nothing at all to help him but they charged him (and got) £1,000 for the privilege.

Debt makes some people crazy while others are happy to live with it - until it catches up with them. If you and your partner have different ways of managing things, keep your finances separate. If necessary, both of you should get some debt counselling. Differing attitudes over money can lead to couples splitting up. They say that love flies out through the window when poverty comes in through the door and there is truth in this. A relationship has to be extremely strong to withstand periods of poverty and debt.

Other considerations

There are governmental benefits to which you may be entitled, such as Working Tax Credit, Family Tax Credit and even income support during a time of crisis. Consult the Citizens Advice Bureau about this. We can't go into all these here, but it would be worth your while to pick up all the booklets that you can find in your local post office, visit the Social Security benefits office, consult the CAB or look up tax credits on the Internet. There are many people around who don't take advantage of these benefits because they don't know about them, because the form filling is daunting or because they are too proud to ask for help. We all pay taxes and National Insurance, and some of this becomes available for our benefit when times are hard. If you hate form filling, enlist the help of a friend who is good at it. We know one family of older people who turned their noses up at extra money that they sorely needed. We also know of two people whose earnings were very low while they were setting up their business, who were able to claim a little extra via the working tax credit scheme.

If you have children and your ex-spouse is not contributing towards their upkeep, contact the Child Support Agency and ask them to chase your ex. We have a funny story about this. A friend of ours divorced her stingy husband and a few weeks later, she received a letter and some forms from the Child Support Agency to check on whether her children were being properly cared for. She pointed out to the agency that her children were in their late twenties, working and married with children of their own, so they were way beyond the stage at which they needed her help. She said that despite the fact that she herself had very little money to spare, she still bought them the odd piece of clothing and gift when she could because she loved them!

Top tips

~ Generally speaking, it is wise to clear your debts before you start to save money, but you may need to keep some savings in hand, so you need to balance this.

~ Even if you are absolutely skint, do buy decent food, because eating rubbish will make you feel weak, tired and prone to sickness.

Jan's comments on mortgage debt

Worm or beetle – drought or tempest – on a farmer's land may fall,
Each is loaded full of ruin but a mortgage beats 'em all!
17th century saying.

Nedbank, the bank that I worked for in South Africa, was very reluctant to throw someone out of their home if they fell into debt. We would put them on a "nursing" list, which meant that we would talk to the homeowner to find out why they had fallen into debt, and make an effort to find some way of retrieving the situation.

However, probably one of the most important things we did to help our clients - in the *first* place - was to turn down the loan application if we felt that the *client* was likely to end up with a problem, for any of a number of reasons - even if the bank wasn't at risk.

But, to continue... sometimes the troubled person was not only a homeowner, but also a farmer who had fallen into debt due to something that went wrong in connection with his crop or stock during the course of a particular year. Nedbank would consider stopping the interest payments on the loan and allowing the person to pay a small amount each month off the capital until things picked up once again. This was partly due to social conscience on behalf of the bank, but also as a matter of practicality. A property left empty after the owner has been evicted is liable to be vandalised, and perhaps will not clear the debt when sold, whereas an owner would make an effort to keep the property in good repair.

If a typical bank forecloses on a mortgage, they have to sell the house by auction, and this may take some time. The house will not be sold at its true value, and if this happens during a recession when property prices are falling, the house will lose its value by leaps and bounds. If it is left empty and unattended it will fall into disrepair. The fixtures and fittings and even the front door will be stolen. It will be vandalised and it may become occupied by squatters.

This may not always be the case in Britain, because our financial institutions have different policies. Nevertheless, in times of trouble it is always worth talking to the lender about your position, as they may make some kind of arrangement, and you don't lose anything by trying. If you are able to make some payments regularly, even if only a small sum, you stand a very good chance of being allowed some form of arrangement.

Lending institutions want people to like them, as this will bring more business their way. They are not charitable organisations though, so there is a limit to their generosity. The moral of this story is that in times of trouble you must not take chances with your home, if at all possible. If you have a problem, talk to your lenders – the sooner the better.

Even if the worst happens and someone loses their home, has County Court Judgements made against them, and even if they are finally made bankrupt, they will eventually get straight. The only debt that could definitely land someone in jail is that of unpaid Council Tax. Bankruptcy can take from one to three years to clear, and a home can be rented. In Europe, most people tend to rent their homes; it is the British and Irish who prefer to buy their homes. Losing one's home is an awful situation to contemplate, but it is not the end of the world and not something that is worth committing suicide over. Nothing is, quite frankly. Life is a learning curve, and those who believe in reincarnation understand that trouble is sent to us in order for our souls to learn and to develop. So learn, understand what trouble feels like and stay out of trouble in future, as that way you can be sure that your karma will improve!

8

Investing: Stocks, Shares and Bonds

An ounce of fortune is worth a pound of forecast.
17th century proverb.

Now here are a few thoughts about the stock market

~ Money invested in the stock market has produced an average return of 9.5% over the past 100 years.

~ The stock market has lost 37% of its value over the past few years.

~ Dot com companies have lost almost all the (false) value that they were quoted at over the past three years.

~ The stock market is showing signs of recovering at the moment, but who knows what it will do next? Is it just a temporary lull before the storm?

So, before we delve into the dizzy heights of wearing red braces and shouting, "Buy, buy, buy," into a telephone, we will explain things in simple terminology, so that you understand every part of what we are talking about in this chapter. We can hear your sighs of relief from here!

Savings and investments

Savings and investments are areas that overlap, but they are not quite the same. As we have seen, savings can include anything from putting pennies into a piggy bank to putting pounds into accounts of various kinds. Investing has a whiff of gambling about it, so it can be a chancy affair.

An investment portfolio

The original "portfolio" was a folder or bag that was divided into sections so that papers (folios) could be carried around (trans*port*ed). Artists keep their work in a special portfolio. An investor needs an imaginary portfolio that contains a variety of investments, and this is called an *investment portfolio*. The idea here is that one should have a *spread* of savings and investments, and not put all one's eggs into one basket.

Here is some jargon just made to confuse you

Imagine that Grandma gave you £5,000. At this moment in time, your best bet might be to purchase a mini cash ISA and to put the rest in a postal or telephone deposit account (these are banking accounts that accept only postal or telephone transactions; this saves costs that are passed on (partly...) to the customer).

Another good idea would be to buy into a tracker unit trust that invests in the FTSE 350. Have we lost you yet?

Possibly we have – and that is part of the problem. The jargon that is used makes investments difficult to understand. So now let us try to unravel some of these terms so that you know what you are trying to achieve with your cache of money.

A bedtime fairy story

Once upon a time, there was a Prime Minister called John Major. Now John Major had once been Chancellor of the Exchequer - and at some point way back before that, he had worked as a bank manager. This meant that he had a better grasp of what ordinary people needed than other Chancellors of the Exchequer who served us, both before and since his day. While working in this job, John Major introduced two straightforward savings schemes for ordinary people - one was called TESSA and the other was called PEP. Both of these allowed people to save up to a certain amount each year in a scheme where their money grew. Unlike other schemes, the profit on these was not taxed.

Now we have Gordon Brown. He is known to be a clever man, but he has never worked as a bank manager and neither has he run a business of his own. Gordon Brown closed down the plain and simple schemes that John Major introduced and instead he has given us the hugely complicated ISA. Furthermore, a large part of the tax advantages of these ISAs falls away with effect from April 2004.

No, dear, we don't understand the logic of all this, either...

ISAs – Individual Savings Accounts

As we all know, rules change, rates change and Chancellors of the Exchequer change. This then is the scene as it is at the time of writing, but it might not be by the time you buy this book. Bear in mind that different institutions may have slightly different rules or arrangements, so if you are seriously considering saving in any kind of ISA, look around to see what is on offer. Many institutions offer ISAs, including banks, the Post Office and even well known retail and other outlets.

An ISA is a scheme that allows you to put money into a spread of investments. It is best viewed as a medium or long-term investment (e.g. five years or more).

If you are an adult, you can save up to £7,000 a year in an ISA. Husbands and wives can each have their own ISA, so a couple can invest £14,000 a year.

You need to be over 16 to save in a cash ISA and over 18 to save in any other kind of ISA.

Any money that you make from an ISA is tax-free, so you don't need to enter any profits from this on a tax form. If you use an accountant for any purpose, it is always worth telling him about your ISAs but he won't put this on your tax form.

NB: After April 2004, part of your profit from your ISA will be taxed! As things stand at the time of writing, if some part of the ISA is invested in shares and if those shares pay a dividend (a bonus), the dividend will be taxed.

An ISA has an annual allowance, so if you have not taken up your full allowance during any tax year, you can't go back and shove more into one that you already have. You can only do this if you bought your ISA during the current tax year and as long as you have under £7,000 (£14,000 for a couple) already in it.

The tax year runs from midnight at the start of the 5th of April in one year to midnight at the end of the 5th of April in the following year. This means that if you make a New Year resolution on the 1st of January to save in ISAs, you and your spouse could each save £7,000 up to the 5th of April and a further £7,000 on the 6th of April – thus saving a total of £28,000 between you over two tax years.

You can put in lump sums or you can save on a monthly basis, as long as this is within the maximum amount that is allowed. You can save a small sum, such as £25 per month.

Even if you are already saving in a TESSA, you can still save up to the maximum in an ISA.

NB: There are no new TESSAs as this scheme has been abandoned, but those who have existing TESSAs can continue to save in them.

If you wish to roll a matured TESSA into an ISA, you can do so as long as you do it within six months of the TESSA maturing. A matured TESSA may have as much as £15,000 in it, so do not cash it in but get the investment company to transfer it for you as then you will have the whole amount in your ISA.

Mini and Maxi ISAs

Here are some details about ISAs (as at end 2003):

~   Every adult is allowed to start up to three Mini ISAs OR one Maxi ISA per year. You have to decide whether you want a Mini or a Maxi ISA in any one year, because you cannot have both during the same year.

~ You can invest up to £3,000 a year in a Mini cash ISA and up to £3,000 a year in a Mini stocks and shares ISA and you can invest £1,000 a year in a Mini ISA that holds insurance bonds (see note below). For the non-mathematicians among you, this comes to the magic £7,000 in any one year.

~ You could invest up to £7,000 in a Maxi ISA which could be invested in unit trusts, shares, corporate bonds or Government gilt edged stock. Alternatively you could choose to put up to £3,000 of your Maxi ISA in cash deposits and the remainder in unit trusts (see more about these in a moment).

Unit trusts

Unit trusts are a worthwhile form of investment even in uncertain times - as long as you are prepared to put your money away in the medium to long term, e.g. for at least five years. At the very least, someone is spending all day every day managing the trust's investments, which is something neither you nor I can do. At the moment, be cautious - it is not clear whether or not the markets have bottomed out, and they probably haven't.

Unit trusts are funds that can be invested in a wide range of assets, including shares, corporate bonds and Government gilt edged stock. The spread of funds is selected by professional fund managers who offer two advantages to the small saver. Firstly they (should) know what they are doing with your money. Secondly they batch your money together with the money that comes in from all the other investors in their scheme. This means that it will make far more out of the situation than if you had simply bought a few shares yourself, and the charges are far less than if you invested as an individual via an agent or a broker.

You don't have to buy into the same fund year after year, you can leave your investment in one fund one year and choose another one the following year, or you can close the ISA off after a year and then open another one with a different company. The real value of this kind of saving is gained by leaving it where it is over a period of years.

Tip

Always check on the charges that will be made by any investment advisor or company at the start of your period of investment, during it (if any) and when you come to sell it again. Check out a number of these and choose the one that is run by the least greedy and rapacious advisor or company.

Cash ISAs

The rate of interest on this can be better than you can gain by saving in a bank or building society.

If you invest in a cash ISA, you can take your money out pretty quickly if you need it again.

NB: A so-called *instant* withdrawal can actually mean within seven working days.

If you want a higher return for your savings, choose a scheme where you can only take your money out by applying and then waiting 30 or 90 days.

CATs

Consider choosing a cash ISA with CAT standards (Costs, Access and Terms), as these are supposedly a little safer than other types, which are mainly stock market based. With a CAT scheme, you can deposit or withdraw as little as £10 per time and you must be able to retrieve your savings within seven working days. The interest rate must be no lower than two per cent below the Bank of England base rate. There are a few more details that you can find out about CATs if you wish, but this covers the basics.

Jan's comment

If you decide to buy an ISA each year, buy a different kind each time round – say, a cash ISA one time, a mixed ISA the next and a stock market one another time. Another good idea is to drip feed money into your ISA on a monthly basis, especially if all or part of it will land up in stocks and shares. The idea here is that if you have all your money in a share or unit trust and that goes down, you could take a considerable loss. Drip feeding means that while share prices are low, the same amount of money buys you more shares, so eventually your average price for the shares you hold improves and your portfolio is bigger than if you had not drip fed the money in.

Gilt edged bonds

We have read that gilt edged bonds (or *gilts* are they are often called) get their name from the fact that they are very safe investments which are said to be "as good as gold", but the fact is that many years ago the actual certificates were gilded or gilt around the edges. A gilt-edged bond is a government bond that is invested in Britain itself, so as long as our country doesn't go to the dogs or get invaded by Martians this should be safe.

Traditionally gilts have always been considered a safe investment with a fixed return on the money that is invested. When the stock market is doing well or the interest that one can get from bank and other deposits is high, gilts don't compare well. As the stock market fell during the first three years of the new millennium and investors lost their money, gilts became more interesting to them.

Keep in mind that gilt prices fluctuate in the same way that share prices do, but in the opposite direction - when share prices or interest rates go down, gilt prices go up.

No Capital Gains Tax (CGT) is payable on profits from the sale of gilts.

Jan's comments on gilts

Briefly, a gilt is a bond or a written commitment to pay the holder an amount of money after a specified period – say in ten years time from when it was issued. In the meantime, a fixed rate of interest is paid. So, if the bond issue was today and you bought it at face value, you could have for example, £20,000 worth of gilts, repayable in 2015 and paying you, say, 5% interest per annum. The selling price of the £20,000 (face value) bonds will depend upon how the 5% compares to other investments available. If the rate is attractive in comparison (as at present), you could sell your holding for more than the £20,000 that you paid for it originally.

In general, people look to gilts when they are uncertain about the safety of the stock market and other fluctuating types of investment, or if they feel that interest rates are likely to drop for some time.

Sasha's comments on gilts
If you understood that lot, you are doing extremely well. Perhaps now you can explain it to me? Alternatively, you can allow your ISA manager to put part of your ISA into gilts and let him worry about the details. Fund managers do this kind of thing every day, so they know what's what.

Corporate bonds

These are similar to gilts but they are not issued by the government, so they aren't quite as safe an investment. You can buy and sell these, but this requires stock market savvy, so these bonds are beyond the scope of this book. They are as safe as the corporation issuing the bond; mostly pretty safe during good times, but not so safe when times are tough.

Savings bonds

These differ from corporate bonds. Anyone over the age of 16 can buy a savings bond via the National Savings scheme at Post Office, and there are other institutions that also make savings bonds available..

You can choose to buy a savings bond for a period of time which may be three, five or ten years.

Bonds have a fixed rate of interest for the duration of the bond.

You can cash savings bonds in early if you need the money, but you will lose some of the interest as a result.

You can choose to leave the interest to pile up in your bond or you can draw it out monthly or annually. It is best to let it accumulate.

The National Savings bond's interest is calculated daily. (Weh hey! Jan approves of that one!)

National Savings allows you to start with an investment of £500; building societies, banks and others may want £1,000 for starters.

The National Savings scheme allows you to invest a total of £1 million; other institutions may offer a higher limit.

A Treasury deposit

You buy these through a bank or from the Bank of England direct, but they require a lump sum of £10,000 or more. These are short-term investments, very safe, but the amounts of money you need to deal with mean that you should have a lot more savvy than this book can provide in order to gain the most out of this kind of investment.

Guaranteed equity bonds

These ensure that at least the nominal amount of the bond is safe - usually, however, excluding a stock market crash or fall. As with all exposures to the stock market, you can lose money on the price at which you buy the bond. There are different features to different bonds, so check the choices available when you are looking to buy.

There are usually heavy penalties for cashing in the bonds early, but there are still enough advantages to make these interesting.

Tip

Keep things simple - we have said this time and again, because it is very important when dabbling in the markets. Institutions don't help when they use different names for products that you may not be interested in, and even using truly contradictory language to tempt you. Look at these examples taken from typical adverts we have come across recently, and you will see how you can easily misunderstand things:

"A Capital protected growth plan". Is this a guaranteed equity bond? It appears to be, from other clues in the advert; why not actually tell us what it is?

"Stock market-linked growth plus a 100% money back assurance" The 100% guarantee sounds appealing nowadays, when the markets are volatile. But read the proviso further down: "In the unlikely event of any issuing institution being unable to meet their financial obligations, *you may not receive back your original investment*". (our italics). Does this gel with the 100% money back assurance? Either something is 100% or it isn't!

One of the problems with keeping your investments safe is the habit of various high street institutions to *massage*, shall we say, unpalatable information.

Don't assume things. You must be, shall we say, *120% certain* that what you *think* is so, actually is so...

Read all the small print. There is always an important reason for the small print message and it *may* hurt you. Double check anything that isn't totally clear.

Stocks and shares

When the stock market is doing well (a bull run), investing in it can be a sensible form of saving. If invested wisely, your money can appreciate in value much more than by any other form of saving. You will normally receive a dividend (like a bonus) twice a year and the value of your investment may go up. In good times, this is a great way to make money, but when the stock market - or the particular company whose shares you hold - is not doing well, you can also lose money. Unless you know exactly what you are doing, it may be preferable to invest in a unit trust fund, although even these don't give you total safety; at least, the fund manager spends all his time looking after the fund's investments, which you can't do yourself. Some funds invest only in British stocks while others invest in a mix of British and overseas stocks, and there are a multitude of other investment options to choose from. It is a fact that money invested in the stock market over a long period will usually do much better than safer forms of investment. You do have to decide at present whether you feel the stock market has reached bottom or not. Our view is that this is not certain and there are enough negative factors to make one lean towards holding back. When there is a really definite upswing, agreed by most of the experts, that's worth waiting for. This is not the case so far.

As with many other forms of investment, you don't need to put a lump sum into shares, as you can drip feed money in on a monthly basis. This spreads the risk, because if you put in a lump sum when the stock market is high and the price of shares fall, your lump will shrink. By drip-feeding, you may lose money on the shares that you bought early in the scheme, but then find yourself able to buy more shares when the market is lower. The idea is that you might lose on the swings but gain on the roundabouts. You need more detailed advice than we are able to give you in this book if you are going to invest in the stock market.

Remember that there is always a charge when you buy or sell shares. You can use a broker or you can use your bank. Brokers can also advise you or choose your shares for you, and their fees vary according to what they do on your behalf. Remember that your gains will be taxed, either as income tax or capital gains tax, so read books on this subject and take lots of advice before doing anything.

Tracker investments

Tracker is a new buzzword that is used in conjunction with some ISAs, unit trusts and other forms of investment. The tracker either tracks the performance of the top 100 companies in the Financial Times Share Index (FTSE or Footsie 100) or the top 350 companies (FTSE 350). This can be a good form of investment even in uncertain times such as these (as long as you know what you are doing and aren't greedy), and it can make much more money over a period of years than any other form of investment. Take advice from a variety of sources and read all the literature before plunging in, as even knowledgeable people can lose a lot of money in the stock market. Don't invest more than you can afford to lose, and always have a basket of investments, not just shares.

A trip to the pet shop, the farm and the zoo

Finally, we have already met *cats* (CATs) but you might be interested to know that a *bull* market is one that is going up and a *bear* market is one that is going down. (Bull *up* and bear *down*). A *stag* is a person who applies for new issues of shares in the hope that within a short period after issuance the price will rise and he will be able to sell at a sizeable profit. Another type of investor is called a *bed and breakfaster,* because he buys shares one day and sells them the next, thus making a quick turnaround.

A *rabbit* is a share that stock traders consider out of the ordinary but it is one that they take a fancy to. It may be a small share that only requires a small investment. The point is that the rabbit hops along and makes a quick profit for the share trader, so he sells it quickly again before bunny hops back into the woods. A *dead cat that bounces* is a share that is low-priced but which suddenly leaps up in price. Lastly, one should try to avoid buying a real *dog* of an investment, such as the much vaunted dot com companies turned out to be!

9

Investing: The Chancy Stuff

A fool and his money are soon parted.
16th century proverb.

Shares in a private business

Your friend Fred decides to open a business and he asks
you to invest in it. What happens after this depends upon a
number of variables, including how well Fred does and the
contract or arrangement that you have with him in the first
place. This is a risky type of investment as there are so
many unforeseen problems that can arise with a small
private business. Business angels are professional business
investors who supposedly know what they are doing.
Sometimes angels will even invest in a stage play or some
other artistic or creative venture.

Standing as guarantor for a business

This is very risky and it is more dangerous than a
straightforward lump sum investment. There is a tendency

to commit yourself to a much higher amount than if you invested a set sum of money. You become totally dependent upon the person or the business that you are guaranteeing, and you have no recourse or say in whatever happens. You would need to come to a separate arrangement as to what benefit you might earn by standing as guarantor.

If you are daft enough to stand as guarantor for anyone (even for your nearest and dearest), ensure that the amount that you guarantee is limited to a sum that you are prepared to lose. If you sign an *unlimited* guarantee, you could end up losing everything you own and more. Jan knew someone who had the unfortunate experience of seeing the bailiffs take her goods and her home after she had stupidly given an unlimited guarantee to a friend. Sasha can remember a man who did this and who even had to take his watch from his wrist and give it to the bailiffs.

The Alternate Investment Market (AIM)

Let's get this one out of the way, right away. In times of uncertainty, forget this kind of investment. Completely. The AIM consists of companies that don't have a normal, formal stock exchange listing, they are listed on a separate stock exchange list, and for one reason or another, they are not as sound as the bigger companies with a proper listing. The risk factor is too high, although the returns may sometimes produce outstanding results, both in dividends and capital growth. The trouble is, of course, you can't tell for certain which of the companies will produce such magic results. You could lose your shirt here, and even in good times, you should never put more into the AIM than you can safely lose.

The property market

Anyone who has bought property as an investment over the past seven years has made a real killing. Property prices are still rising in many areas at the time of writing, albeit more slowly than of late, but some more expensive or overpriced properties in some areas are beginning to fall back. If deflation kicks in, property may slump, but if interest rates fall again in order to stimulate industry or to match the lower rates in the EU and USA, it may rise even further. This is obviously an area of investment that is unsuitable unless you are really knowledgeable about property investments.

Perhaps now is a good time for property barons to crystallise some or all of their gains, by selling some of their properties. This way, if there is a property slump, it won't affect the profit made on a sold property. Naturally, there would be CGT to take into account. Two of the choices to make are whether a (major) slump would result in a bigger loss than paying up CGT, and whether current tenant rentals would be really stable in a recession.

At times, you can buy property, do nothing at all to it other than to hang on to it until the price rises and then sell it. You can renovate a property and sell it, but take care not to spend more than is necessary on the renovations. You can buy property and let it out. This can be a private matter or you can allow a letting agency handle this for you.

All these ideas are fraught with potential problems and we haven't even started to look at the differences between private and commercial mortgages, and income tax issues, so you can see that this needs much investigation before you jump in. Having said this, if the most you can get for your money anywhere else is peanuts, even a small rise in the price of property over a period of a year or more makes it a good investment, not least because of *gearing*. Gearing simply refers to the fact that you only put down a fraction of the price of the property and take a mortgage for the remainder. This leads to the fact that, if you are switched on and well-off, it is possible to buy two or three properties, spending only the price of one, and renting them out to cover most if not all the amount of the combined mortgage repayments.

If you are clever at building, decorating, gardening, renting and a number of other linked skills, this is a thought – but it is not a good idea for the uninitiated person to jump at. Remember - property prices rose sharply in the 1980s and then fell like a stone in the early 1990s - and the same may (or may not) happen again. Property prices do rise over the long-term though, so, provided you have *a lot of cash* available to tide you through cashflow problems, it is certainly possible to do well out of property. We can't go more deeply into property investments and speculation here; there are so many things to cover that they warrant whole books on their own.

Your own home

Your own home is *not* an investment, it is a place to live and be happy in. Sure, keeping it in good order, adding bits and pieces and improving it can only help when you come to sell it and move on. You should really look at it as your haven rather than as a get-rich-quick type of enterprise. Before you do too much work on your house, consider whether you are pricing it out of the local market and whether it might not be better to move to a larger house. In other words, if the other properties in your street are worth / selling for up to say, £150,000 you won't get £250,000 for yours, no matter how many gold-plated taps and doorknobs you put in...

Jan's words on property

The real market value of a property is the amount of money that a willing buyer is prepared and able to pay a willing seller.
Jan Budkowski

The view from a house may be very attractive, and may well ensure a higher price in good times, when people can afford to pay more for such "niceties". When times get hard, the view becomes a luxury and is not worth anything – only things such as the size of the house, scarcity in the area, its condition and proximity to schools will mean something to a buyer.

A safer method of investing in property is in a property trust. These are similar to stock market unit trusts but they concentrate on commercial properties. This way you gain the expertise of people who deal in properties all day and every day, and who are more likely to succeed in investing the trust's portfolio wisely. They are not infallible, so make sure, as with any other investment route, that the institution is a sound, stable one with a good track record. Don't just sign up with a new organisation. Never – I repeat, never be attracted just because there is a free kettle or camera offered as an enticement, or if the company offers to make no charges for a month. Very often, the small enticement is offered because the institution is not making progress due to a poor track record.

The value of a property is not what the estate agent says it should be, it is not what the buyer paid for the next-door property, it is not even the amount you paid for it one month ago. Ultimately, it is not even the property size or number of gold taps in the four bathrooms. It is what an interested person is able or prepared to pay to an interested seller. This means, naturally, that a property commands a higher price when money is readily available, and a lower price when money is tight, because buyers will not be prepared (or able) to pay as much as the seller would like.

A further consideration, therefore, is that you should make every effort to avoid being in a position where you might have to sell the property in a downturn. This is something that too many people let themselves in for. I have had clients come to me with sad tales of how their string of properties that they had bought with the intention of renting out so that they could live off the income had turned into a veritable basket of woes. You must have a sizeable cushion in your financial planning to allow you an uninterrupted cash-flow, even in times of low or no rentals, and it is surprising how many otherwise very sensible people have come a cropper this way.

Gold

Gold is probably the best-known investment commodity. It is also known as a *hard asset* or *hard commodity*. Gold has the following attributes:

The for's

~   It doesn't rust, deteriorate and it has no sell by date.
~   It is easily stored, physically small in size.
~   It is a sound store of value in times of uncertainty and war.
~   It is internationally accepted in various forms – e.g. coins, jewellery and ingots.
~   The best form in which to invest in gold physically is in coins – not "proof" coins, as the value of these depends more on their rarity value to a collector – just consider normal gold coins, such as the South African Krugerrand, British Sovereign, US Gold Eagle or Canadian Gold Maple Leaf.
~   VAT is no longer payable on gold coins in the UK.

Gold has definitely shown a marked level of appreciation in value over the last couple of years, largely because of global fears about the chances of recession, deflation, war and terrorism. Similarly, with stock markets performing badly, more stability is now perceived in gold. It doesn't earn interest but it is not likely to lose value in the foreseeable future, so it is more attractive nowadays.

The againsts

~   Gold is very heavy for its size – if you keep a hoard of ingots in the attic, your ceiling might collapse!
~   As with commodities, gold earns you no interest or dividends; you have to hope for appreciation in value over time for any gains. Gold has not done well for decades, because other investments have been able to give a much better return on your investment.

~ There tend to be restrictions in the movement of gold between different countries. Rules and legislation that apply today will not necessarily be the same in a few years time, even in the UK, although the present position is quite flexible.

~ In the form of jewellery, you are paying a lot of money for the work involved in addition to the seller's profit margin. If you sell jewellery, you are unlikely to get more than half of what you paid for it.

Jan's comments

I have had clients in Zimbabwe who even invested in goldmines, which is probably one of the more extreme examples I have come across. Nevertheless, I would not exclude this as an investment - but only if the person knew exactly what he was doing. Two of my "gold diggers" were accountants by trade. They had dollar signs in their eyeballs as big as their egos. An accountant (or a banker, or a cobbler or whatever) may know something about what comes out of a mine, but what it takes to get it out is another story. The outcome (as you may expect) was a total write-off.

Jewellery, stamps, coins, antiques and so on

These are classed as *collectibles*, and each has its own good and bad points from an investment point of view. As with many other forms of investment, these items are best held for at least 5 years in order to see any useful appreciation. It is also wise to insure them for their full value, even though this may be costly. If you don't insure the goods for their full value, you will very likely have a problem with the insurance company in the event of a loss or robbery. Read the small print in your insurance policy.

Jewellery

From an investment point of view, make sure that you don't pay too much for the workmanship as opposed to the content. Make sure that bits don't come off easily, e.g. diamonds coming loose from their mountings. Even with a good deal, it is likely that you will not be able to sell jewellery for anywhere near what you paid for it, unless there is something really exceptional about it.

While it is perfectly possible to sell the odd unwanted item of jewellery and so on to a pawnshop when times are rough, it is another thing to trade in these things or even to *appear* to trade in such items. In this case, care must be taken or both income tax and capital gains tax might be levied. If you sell valuable family heirlooms, anything over a limit of £6,000 brings capital gains tax into play. The tax will be levied on the whole price of the goods, not just the part that is over £6,000.

Oddly enough, this doesn't apply to medals for valour or gallantry, even if the vendor is not the person who won them or related in any way to that person. Certain items are considered to be a "wasting asset", i.e. one that has a shelf life of no more than 50 years. Thus vintage wine and machinery such as clocks, cameras and barometers come into this category. There are many more rules, regulations and exemptions that apply to this kind of trade – not the least of them the new rules that are coming in to counteract money laundering – so specialist advice will be needed here.

Stamps

Buy top quality stamps – don't go for just good quality. Stamps must be handled very carefully and never with your fingers. If you don't already know exactly how to treat stamps, buy one of the many books that will teach you. Keep them in proper stamp albums and don't mount them on hinges, not even if they are used stamps. Keep your stamps in a dry place, safe from damp and also from insects and vermin, or you will find a rat in your collection box and no stamps…

Coins

As with stamps, buy top quality, don't ever handle them with your fingers, keep them in proper coin albums, and buy yourself a book unless you are already very knowledgeable about coin collecting. It may be a good idea to keep your investment collection in safe keeping at the bank.

Antiques

You must know a lot about the subject if you are to invest in antiques. A book is not enough because you will really need more than that to ensure you buy really good items. Each different kind of antique will need different kinds of attention, from the right polish, environment and temperature for furniture, to safe packing or display cabinets for delicate china and glassware. We can't cover everything you need to know in this book, we can only suggest that you must take great care before spending money on antiques.

NB: *Note from Sasha.* I listened to a program on the radio yesterday on just this subject and it said that English watercolour paintings are going up in value. Furniture is not a good investment right now and clocks are a waste of time. So now you know!

Fine wine

Although this is a fascinating hobby, wine is best used to accompany a meal. There is just too much involved in keeping wine as an investment – a decent cellar and a cool, stable, dark environment are just the start. Enjoy drinking the wine instead!

Paintings and other artistic or rare collectibles

Again, here you are delving into esoteric depths unless you are really knowledgeable about the specific items. These are much too involved for this book and for that matter, for normal investment purposes. In general, our mottos are along the lines of:

~ Keep it simple.
~ Don't be greedy.
~ There's no such thing as a free lunch.
~ Unbelievable opportunities are exactly that – unbelievable.

That way, you can't go far wrong. Don't let people entice you with incredible offers. Don't be turned on by exotic forms of losing your money swiftly, such as shares in Kiwi fruit plantations. You just don't get far by taking risks you can't afford, and tempting opportunities abound exactly when you should be most careful: that is, when times are hard and when uncertainty abounds.

One feature to remember is that the important aspects of any collectible or commodity are its tangible, genuinely realizable attributes. For example, gold has a physical value that is pretty stable. If it is in the form of a rare coin, the added value is as a collectible item. There are people who are prepared to pay more for the coin simply to have it in their collection, and they have to compete with others who have the same idea. If, however, money becomes short, then people are less able to afford their collecting hobbies, so rare coin prices may well drop. The same applies to stamps and antiques.

In short, with all these items, you need to know exactly what you're doing when using them as investments.

Whatever line you are in, in uncertain times, *cash is king!* Just ask the South African cattle baron, worth over R40,000,000 who lost it all because he ran out of cash at a time when cattle weren't selling at all during an extended period of drought, and his whole empire was appropriated in lieu of repayment of his very large bank loans and other debts.

The story of the Aztec artefact
We can all do daft things at times and even bankers can be extremely silly on occasion, as you will see from the following story.

At one point, Jan took over the management of a branch of Nedbank in South Africa. While looking around his new domain, he found a rather nice "thingy" sitting in the vault. It was a wooden plaque about a meter high by a third of a meter wide, and it was made to hang on a wall. It had three circles of green stone in it, each containing some kind of South American figure. When Jan asked one of the staff about it, they told him that a client had given the plaque to the bank as security against a large loan. He had told them that it was a genuine Aztec artefact and that it was definitely valued at US$100,000, which was certainly more than enough to cover the loan. One wonders why the manager of the day didn't suggest to the client that he sell the plaque and not bother with the loan in the first place. Anyway, the hapless manager took the plaque, gave the man the large loan and stuffed the poor "thingy" into the vault without getting it formally valued. Needless to say, the man defaulted on the loan and the artefact turned out to be far from Aztec - and far from valuable.

Jan knew that the plaque was clearly valueless, but he liked the look of it, so he asked someone higher up in the organisation if he could have it for himself, and he paid a small amount for it. This plaque is one of the few things that Jan has managed to salvage from his previous life in South Africa, and it is happily gracing a wall in our house. We both love it; and we love the story behind it too. We have not had our "thingy" valued, but if it turned out that the bits of stone and the tatty pieces of red cloth that cover part of the wood *are* actually worth something, we will both feel unbelievably daft. Naturally, we would laugh all the way to the bank – and ask for a large loan, of course!

A really safe investment

By buying this book, you will surely save money - and you may even make some too. As long as you take plenty of advice and don't plunge into anything without reading all the literature that you can find, you may not make a fortune, but you should make *something* and at least have a bit put by for a rainy day. Remember that things change rapidly in the world of finance. Although the information in this book is of a general nature, things may change by the time that you wish to use it, so do ensure that you check everything out before taking action. Good luck!

When Sasha and I are fed up, tired and under pressure, I usually threaten to pack up the publishing business and buy a chicken farm. This (as Sasha knows full well) is my idea of another silly and totally illogical move – a lifelong banker switching to raising chickens! Mind you, maybe if I bought a book about it… Nah, my soft-hearted Sasha could never bring herself to part with any of the chickens, let alone kill or eat any of them. We would end up with a yard full of expensive pets!

10

Income, Outgoings and Outcome

If it ain't in black and white, it don't exist.
Jan Budkowski

This chapter covers the one thing that everybody hates doing, but it has to be done if you are to stand any chance of getting your finances under control. So let us all bite the bullet, grasp the nettle, put our noses to the grindstone, our shoulders to the wheel, our best foot forward, our backs and our hearts into it - and pretend we are chancellors of our own exchequers!

If you ran a small business or became self-employed, the first thing you would learn is to get into the habit of keeping every receipt, credit card slip or bill that comes your way. You would then sift through them and see which could conceivably apply to your particular business so that you could put them against your annual tax bill. In this chapter, we are suggesting that you start to think in this businesslike manner, not so much to save on tax as for your own peace of mind.

A budget for a week

List all the money that comes in for one week, and on a separate sheet of paper list every single penny that you spend during that week. This will give you some idea of what's going on.

A budget for a month

This is the same procedure as the weekly budget, but it will give you an even clearer idea of your spending habits. Once you have done this, you will be able to see where you can make budget cuts or where you need to set more aside for emergencies. You may even come to the conclusion that you need to take an extra "moonlight" job for a while, until you can get your finances back into shape again.

In particular, list all direct debits. These may be a cheaper way to pay certain bills, but they sweep out of your bank account without you noticing, so ensure that you know exactly what your direct debit list is costing you each month and allow for it.

A budget for a year

Do a budget for one month and see if that covers all the usual things on which you spend money and then multiply this by twelve. Add those things that don't come up each month - such as household repairs, annual bills, car tax and insurance, holidays, Christmas and birthdays. Also add any income that comes in less often than monthly. Once you have done this you will see how much money you have left each year (or how much shortfall you need to make up). Then it is much easier to decide how much you should be able to save (and *do* save it; put away a portion every week or month, as money comes in).

On the other hand, your income may be less than your expenses. On an annual summary, the shortfall may well look frightening, or even impossible to correct. Well, nine times out of ten, it isn't, and don't dwell on the annual picture. Divide the shortfall by twelve and concentrate on this figure instead. This way, it will be much more feasible to find ways of dealing with it, either by cutting down expenses, increasing income, or both.

Income list

The following is a suggested list of incoming monies; ignore what doesn't apply and add those things that do.

Wages or salary

Benefits and pensions

Extra earnings

Rebates and bonuses

Interest on savings

Help from relatives

Sundry extras

A monthly shopping list

The rest of this chapter will be devoted to a huge shopping list, which you can fill in according to your income and outgoings. You will find many items that don't apply and several that we haven't thought of, so just ignore those that don't apply and add more as necessary. Don't worry about pennies, just round everything up to the nearest pound.

Monthly expenses are easy to work out but if there are some things that you pay annually, you will need to divide these by twelve. You probably don't buy things like furniture or garden equipment very often, so just estimate how much you spend on these things in a year and divide by twelve. Then build up a reserve fund for such large or unusual items and also for potential replacement of appliances and other things that are nearing the end of their lifespan.

Your house

Mortgage
Mortgage insurance
Building and contents insurance
Rent
Maintenance charges
Council tax
Electricity, gas, water
TV, licence, rental, cable, satellite
Telephone, Internet charges
Hire Purchase
Rented equipment
Large items (furniture, appliances)
Small items (kitchen goods, small radio etc.)
Tools
Repairs and renewals
Decorating
Household goods
Cleaning and window cleaning
Gardening, gardener
Sundries

Vehicle

Hire purchase or lease hire
Tax
Insurance
Interest on car loan
MOT, servicing and repairs
Fuel
Sundries

Regular travel

Fares
Books, papers and food on the go

Children

Childcare
Fares
School fees
School lunches
School extras
School holidays
Books and toys
Clothes
Activities and tutors
Entertainment and outings
Haircutting
Sundries

Health

Dental
Optical
Chiropodist

Chiropractor or osteopath
Prescription drugs
Other drugs
Vitamins and supplements
Alternative therapies

Financial

Overdraft and Loan repayments
Credit card repayment
Interest on credit cards
Interest on store cards
Pension
Savings
National Insurance
Tax or extra tax
Repayment of loan to relative

Personal

Catalogue
Clothes
Cosmetics and toiletries
Hairdresser
Dry cleaning
Subscriptions, clubs, societies

Treats

Newspapers, books, magazines
Cigarettes
Booze
Pub and social outings
Days out and visiting friends

Entertaining
Clubbing, bowling, dancing, evening classes
Sports
Cinema, videos, CDs etc.
Going to shows
Holidays and trips
Other

Essentials (for a laugh...)

Chocolate
Perfume
Jimmy Choo shoes
Books from Zambezi Publishing Ltd

11

Home Loans and Mortgages

An Englishman's home is his castle.
Proverb.

Buying a home is likely to be the largest investment that you will make during your lifetime. Even if you move house several times, this is still likely to be the case. Unless you are lucky enough to inherit a house or to inherit enough money to buy one outright, you will doubtless need to apply for a mortgage. Once upon a time, the only place that supplied mortgages was a building society, but now you can get mortgages from banks and other places as well. You could even obtain a loan that is large enough to pay part of the cost of a home.

The price of houses goes up and down. In these uncertain times, prices could go in almost any direction in different parts of the country due to local conditions, but over the long term, houses always rise in value. You have to live somewhere, and as long as you look after your home, it will look after you. House prices don't normally jump about as much in other parts of Europe as they do in the UK, partly because we don't make as much use of long-term fixed rate mortgages as many other EU countries do.

A brilliant idea

Now here is a brilliant idea that doesn't actually exist, but if we had the necessary millions to spare, we would start a business that offered just this service. We call this a *mobile* mortgage, although a better name might be a *transferable* mortgage. The idea is that when a person moves - rather than paying up his mortgage and starting all over again with another one, he takes his mortgage with him. This would have two immediate effects that would benefit both the borrower and the lender. The borrower would not have all the hassle of having to go back and reapply to his lender or starting to look around for another lender, and if he had a fixed rate mortgage he would not incur a penalty due to closing the mortgage. The lender would not run the risk of losing a client who took the opportunity of going somewhere else. Even if the borrower could get a better deal elsewhere, inertia would encourage him to stay with his current lender. As long as the new property was properly surveyed, and as long as the lender was happy to increase the amount or duration of the mortgage on a larger or more expensive home, this should work well. Jan says that this is a perfectly logical concept, which would work on exactly the same basic principle as when the bank takes security against any other kind of loan. After all, if we sell our car and buy ourselves another, we can transfer the insurance from one to the next, so why shouldn't we be able to transfer a mortgage in exactly the same way?

N.B. Lo and behold, while editing this book, we have just come across news of just this kind of mortgage transfer. That means it should not be too long before some of the other banks will have to follow suit, so keep your eyes open, if this is an attractive feature for you.

Choice

There are apparently over 4,000 flavours of mortgage deals on offer, so what you opt for will depend upon your personal circumstances and a bit of help from an independent financial advisor, because you can't investigate all these options and varieties. One thing that you can do, and that we recommend, is to keep things simple. Don't be tempted to go for dazzling offers and cunning ways of doing this or that, or avoiding the other. People thought the endowment mortgage was a great dazzler originally. There are people who did do well with them, some time ago, but tens of thousands of people are now suffering badly with their endowment mortgages, because, to put it simply, your home is not something to speculate with, it is something to try and make as secure as possible.

Basically, mortgages fall into these categories:

Endowment mortgages.

Repayment mortgages.

Interest only mortgages (with some other form of saving attached).

Pension plan mortgages

Flexible mortgages.
Offset mortgages.
Variable rate mortgages.
Fixed rate mortgages.
Self-certificated mortgages.

Endowment mortgages

With this kind of mortgage, you only pay the interest on the mortgage over the years, while you also pay into an endowment policy. The idea is that the endowment policy eventually grows enough to pay off your mortgage when you come to the end of the borrowing period. This is usually something like 20, 25 or 30 years. This used to be considered a very good idea, but this system doesn't seem to work any more. This is due to the fact that the money in the endowment is invested, as most investments are, in the stock market, and in recent years these policies have not grown enough to cover people's mortgages. This means that when the homeowner comes to the end of his mortgage period, the mortgage may be far from paid off. The only thing to do in this case is to extend the mortgage period or change to a repayment basis and pay up for several more years. Endowment mortgages are a problem, many are likely to become problems at some point, and the same problems arose in South Africa some years ago.

Jan cannot recommend endowment mortgages, notwithstanding the fact that many of them have been no problem in the past. As the saying goes in investment adverts that involve the stock market, "past performance is no guarantee of future results".

There are already many thousands of people trapped in these schemes. If you are one of the lucky ones who are still on the right track, think carefully about increasing your monthly repayments or perhaps even changing to a non-endowment mortgage if that option is available without too much of a penalty. Why gamble on the stock market with the roof over your head?

Repayment mortgages

This is exactly what it sounds like. You pay the interest and you also pay off some of the capital off the mortgage as you go along. What you actually pay for most of the time is the interest, only biting into the original debt towards the end of the mortgage period. This is what one might term a "bog-standard" mortgage.

Interest-only mortgages and investment-linked mortgages

Obviously you only pay the interest on this mortgage, but you will have to do something else to cover the loan. So here we are either back to the endowment idea or something similar. This could be in the form of a pension plan that is linked to the mortgage. This may be a good idea, but it strikes us that you might be better off by taking a repayment mortgage and knowing that your loan balance is definitely reducing every month.

One trendy idea is a tracker mortgage. Here, you pay the interest only and another sum that is invested into the stock market. The fund manager tracks the best shares to make your money grow. Under normal circumstances, this is a good idea, but the stock market lost 37% of its value in the first three years of the new millennium. We recently read one account where an analyst worked out that, with a mortgage of £100,000 over 20 years with this scheme, there would be a shortfall of £23,000 at the end of the period. This may be a better deal in future, but should anything as important as your home be tied to the volatile stock market? As we said earlier, do you really want to gamble with the roof over your head?

Flexible mortgages and offset mortgages

These are a new idea in this country, although Jan was used to dealing with them in South Africa when he was in charge of the Home Loans Credit Risk Management department in Nedbank. In South Africa they loosely call these mortgages access bonds, and the idea is that you put money into the mortgage account when you have it to spare, and then take it out again when you need to. You will notice that we warn against borrowing against your home for anything other than home improvements, but if you put extra spare money into the mortgage, you can then take it out again for any purpose. Every time you put money in, you reduce the interest that you ultimately pay, so this will also considerably reduce the term of the mortgage.

This also gives you access to money in times of trouble, and it equates to getting an *after-tax* return on your money equivalent to your mortgage rate. Where else can you get that nowadays?

Financial institutions in this country are not as generous as they are in South Africa, so if you opt for this kind of mortgage, the interest rate may be slightly higher than for a normal repayment mortgage. At the moment, interest rates are low overall, so the extra percentage won't make much difference to your monthly payments, but it might do so if the rates rise further. Nevertheless, this still looks like a good option to us.

Some flexible mortgages lump your current account, savings account or even the entire contents of your larder and underwear drawer into one account. This seems a bit worrying to us, because your circumstances are bound to change over a 20 year period, so what suits you now may not suit you in years to come. Even more to the point, this makes it difficult to work out where exactly you stand, if your loans and credit monies are all mixed into one account.

Some schemes allow you to offset the interest that you make on a savings account against the interest that you pay on the mortgage. Interest rates on mortgages are low, but at the moment the interest on savings plans is pitiful. This may or may not be worth it, but our view is that the offset should be at the mortgage rate, so look into this carefully while you are hunting for the right mortgage.

Variable rate mortgages

This term usually refers to a repayment mortgage, but it could relate to other types as well. The interest on the mortgage usually rises or falls along with the base rate set by the Bank of England. This is 3.5% at the time of writing, which is the lowest it has been for nearly fifty years. Mortgage interest rates historically run at around eight per cent over a couple of decades. At the moment, you can pay anything from under four per cent to almost six per cent interest, depending on the kind of mortgage that you have.

At one time in the mid 1970s, mortgage interest topped 17%, so you need to bear this kind of thing in mind when you decide how much to borrow. Borrow up to the hilt by all means, but bear in mind that your monthly payments could double if the interest rate rose much.

NB: Look up *mortgages* on the Internet and find one or two institutions that allow you to work out what your repayments would be at various different rates of interest. You will then be able to see for yourself what your monthly repayments would come to, at different interest rates.

Fixed rate mortgages

It is quite common for lenders to offer a mortgage at a fixed rate of interest for a couple of years or even for five years at the start of a mortgage. After this initial period the mortgage reverts to a variable rate. Sometimes, the fixed rate may be lower than the variable rate. At a time like now, when interest rates are low, it is a good idea to take a five-year deal like this. The only drawback is that if you decide to move house within the five years, and thus have to pay the mortgage off and start again with a new one, there could be a hefty penalty – even if you stay with the same mortgage lender. Having said this, there are some banks which only charge a relatively small administration fee rather than a large penalty, and it would be wise to ask about this aspect when first considering a fixed rate option. We gather that it is becoming possible with some banks to transfer your mortgage from one property to another, which would be very useful.

In some circumstances, it is possible for a fixed rate mortgage to become a millstone. This is if interest rates fall so much that they fall far below the rate set into the mortgage, which means that you are paying more than anyone else for your mortgage. However, this is the small risk that one takes when opting for a fixed rate, and it is less painful than finding your monthly repayments growing to unmanageable levels.

Self-certificated mortgages

A self-employed person or someone running a private (not a limited) company or working in a partnership can usually get a mortgage if he can show three years healthy trading on his books and his balance sheet. If he cannot show this kind of a profit, or if he has only recently started to trade, he can only get a self-certificated mortgage. There are two downsides. The rate of interest that he will pay is higher than would be the case for a normal variable rate mortgage, but the real bummer is that he must put down as much as 25% of the cost of the house as a deposit. Lenders used to insist on only 15%, but the 25% rate seems to be standard for this type of mortgage lately. This makes sense from the lender's point of view, because this is a risky deal for the company to get into. This way they know that even if house prices drop later, and they have to sell the property at auction at some point, they can't lose much. You will also need to take out mortgage insurance for this kind of deal, and that ensures that the lending organisation won't lose out in cases of disaster.

For the record, mortgage insurance is a good thing in our view, so even if you can get away without it somehow, we suggest that you do take it up. Naturally, check the premiums against those from elsewhere, or you may end up paying too much for the same cover.

Buy-to-let mortgages

These are beyond the scope of this book as they verge on a form of business venture, but if you are interested in this option, check out everything involved very carefully. A flexible mortgage might be a good idea here, as the rent that you receive may be much higher than the mortgage repayments, so every time that the property is being let out, you can shovel the spare cash into it. This will reduce both the cost and duration of the mortgage.

Islamic (Shariah) mortgages

This is now the umpteenth time that we have added something new into our book while doing the final edit before printing! It just shows how quickly things change nowadays, and it confirms our decision to keep this book on general terms, without quoting specific rates, etc. as far as possible. You always need to check on the latest conditions before signing up for anything, especially in the financial arena.

Back to the Shariah mortgage. Islamic law prohibits the charging of interest, so there has always been a problem for an Islamic customer hoping to purchase a property. The banks have not been willing to look at these problems, but it seems that they are starting to do so now. As we have said before, now that one bank is offering a Shariah mortgage, other institutions are sure to follow.

Our view.

This should be a welcome development. Having said that, we have not seen full details of the costs, conditions, etc. and therefore we cannot comment on the specific product. The problem still exists that the bank has to purchase the property itself and then sell or lease it to the customer over the usual twenty or so years. The end result is that two lots of stamp duty may be payable. The government has been looking into these ramifications, but the outcome has yet to materialise. There are many pros and cons to digest; for example, on the one hand, surely it should be possible to make legal provision for one lot of stamp duty in these specific circumstances? On the other hand, even so, what happens if the customer decides - or has to - sell the property before completion of the deal? Is the bank stuck with being a reluctant property owner, which is really not their line of business? Only time will tell the outcome.

Negative equity

If you are young, you may never have heard of negative equity, so let us take you back to the early 1990s for a moment to show you what can happen. In the 1980s, house prices rose sharply, but then the economy went into a nosedive and house prices dropped dramatically. Those who had large mortgages found themselves paying for a property that was now worth much less than the value of the mortgage. This was not pleasant, but as long as those people kept their jobs (and their heads) and waited it out, they found that their home eventually regained its value and then increased once again. However, the recession meant that many people lost their jobs or suffered other financial hardship, and they could not sell their homes and clear the mortgage. There were many stories of people who simply put the keys to their home in the post to the company that lent them the money and just walked away. If they could be found later, they had to pay off the debt or live with a bad credit record and without the ability to borrow anything ever again (even on a credit card). This situation is actually worse than bankruptcy, as that only means not being able to borrow for the next three years at most, while this debt can go on indefinitely.

Council housing, housing associations and controlled tenancies

You may be able to buy the house or flat that you live in outright if you are in a council house, a housing association or if you are in a property under a controlled rent. If so, the property should be considerably cheaper than a private property and it could be worth raising a mortgage for the purpose.

Other data

~ *Never* raise a second mortgage for anything other than improvements to your house.

~ *Never* allow your home to be used to support a guarantee for anything, or to prop up a failing business. Allowing your home to be security for someone else's business or someone else's problems will surely cost you your home and land you with huge debts to boot.

~ You may be asked to insure your mortgage. The idea is that the balance will be paid off if you are sick or if you die, and this is no bad thing (the insurance, not the dying...). The policy that the mortgage lender tries to sell you may not actually do all of this, or it may be expensive compared to other policies, so look around elsewhere and see what kind of alternative policies you can get.

~ Always get a thorough survey on a property before buying it. Ensure that this is better than the basic one, which doesn't really look closely at the property; it just ensures that the property is good enough for the lender's purposes.

~ If you think you are likely to move house again in the reasonably near future, check that you can close your mortgage and take another one (with the same company or with a different one) without having to pay a penalty.

~ If you think you will need to change the kind of mortgage you take out, check that you can do so without incurring penalties.

~ Always find a mortgage where the interest is calculated on your daily balance. This will save you a packet in interest over the years.

~ If you arc refused a mortgage or any other form of finance, look into this and appeal. Supply additional evidence if possible, so that the lender can reconsider. Check your credit records with Experian and Equifax, in case there is a black mark that you may be unaware of.

~ Don't speculate on property to make money unless you know what you are doing.

~ If you rent out a room, watch the tax implications on this.

~ If the base rate (the rate that the Bank of England sets) falls but your interest rate doesn't, ask why. Your rate will go up swiftly if base rate goes up, so the same should apply when it drops.

Our verdict

~ At the present time a mortgage that is fixed for five years at current low rates is probably a good buy, as long as you don't intend to move again during that time.
~ A flexible mortgage could be even better, as long as you check out the rate of interest that is charged and any penalties for closing the account when you move.
~ Don't put all your bank accounts into this type of mortgage, as you might want to do things differently later.

Vernon's story

Vernon bought his house in 1964. The house cost £6,400 and Vernon could put down a deposit of £3,400 so he needed a mortgage of £3,000. That shows just how much property prices have increased in the past 40 or so years!

Vernon looked at the two mortgage options that were available at that time. One was for a variable rate mortgage that was running at 5.5% at the time. The other option was to take a mortgage on a fixed rate of 6% for the whole 20-year period of the mortgage. (Isn't it odd how things change; these days, the interest on a fixed rate mortgage can be lower than a variable rate one, whereas then it was higher. Jan says it all depends on forecasts - the bank has to take a view as to what level it thinks interest rates will be each year down the line, and it sets fixed rates accordingly).

Vernon was a notably stingy character so he opted for the cheaper variable rate mortgage in order to save himself from paying the extra half per cent. The interest rate soon began to rise, and ten years later, it was running at 17%! However, Vernon was lucky in the end, because he had taken out an endowment mortgage of a kind that no longer exists. Vernon paid the interest to the mortgage lender and a separate amount into the endowment policy to cover the capital. When the mortgage period was finished, Vernon's house was his own and he received a bonus of a further £3,000 from the endowment policy. Unfortunately, inflation meant that this bonus payment, which had seemed huge in 1964, was pretty paltry by 1984!

Peter's story

Peter has moved seventeen times. He has bought and sold at good and bad times, he has sometimes made a profit, and at other times he has made a loss. Through these ups and down, including three messy divorces, he has never managed to pay off a mortgage completely and he has had to take yet another new one recently.

Frank's story

Frank went into a dodgy business venture that eventually went bust. He had a 20-year mortgage that was nearing the end of its term, but he used his house to back his guarantee for the business. To clear the sizeable overdraft he had built up, he then had to take out *another* 20-year mortgage, just to stay where he was!

Sam and Frances's story

Sam and Frances bought their current house when prices in their area were just starting to rise. They took a self-certificated repayment mortgage for a period of fourteen years. Now the price of the house has doubled and the mortgage is going down by leaps and bounds. They realise that house prices will drop back again to some extent, but whatever happens, their house is well on the way to being paid for.

Ann and Gus's story

Ann and her Gus moved into their lovely four-bedroom house and set about making improvements and working on the garden. A few weeks later, Gus developed a raging headache that just wouldn't go away. This disconcerted him as he was a fit man and he rarely suffered from headaches. Eventually he went to the doctor only to discover that he had a particularly severe form of cancer. Gus was dead within seven months of moving into his new home. He had taken out insurance against this potentially unlikely event, so Ann had no worries about keeping the home for herself and her children.

Finally...

Interest rates may not stay as low as they are for very much longer. Here are some figures that Jan found on the Internet via the Council of Mortgage Lenders, which we applied to a mortgage of £50,000 over 11 years. The details worked out as follows:

Interest only mortgage at 5% interest – monthly payment:	£208.33
Repayment mortgage at 5% interest – monthly payment:	£501.62
Interest only mortgage at 10% interest – monthly payment:	£416.66
Repayment mortgage at 10% interest – monthly payment:	£641.51

In 1977 the mortgage interest rate was 17%! Even a small mortgage could become impossible if rates rise to those levels again. Worse still, when times are tough, banks and credit card companies will be less ready to lend money, so consider what difficulties such uncertain times could bring... The answer is, as usual, simply don't over-extend yourself with massive mortgages, and build up and keep available a sensible level of cash reserve that can cope with at least six month's worth of unexpected expenses.

In uncertain times, there is only one way to end this chapter. You know the health warning on cigarette packs, the one that we never bother thinking about. Well, there is also one, by law, on mortgage loan adverts. The reason for it is to help prevent the kind of problem that has happened so often in the past. Ignore the cigarette packs, by all means, but please think about the mortgage one and pay off your mortgage, the sooner the better:

"Your home is at risk if you do not keep up payments on a mortgage or other loan secured on it".

12

Renting a Home

Murphy's Golden Rule:
Whoever has the gold makes the rules.

In Europe, home ownership is far less common than it is here; many people rent their homes. Obviously there are many property owners who make a living out of the rents that they receive. In Britain, anybody will tell you that it is far better to buy your own place than to pay rent to a landlord. Renting a place is like pouring money down the drain – and it is someone else's drain into the bargain! However, there are exceptions to every rule, and a case for renting property in some circumstances; for example:

~ Council tenants.
~ Students.
~ Young people who are embarking on a new relationship and who are not sure that it will last.

~ People who are only likely to stay in a country or an area for a short period of time.
~ Those who cannot afford a deposit on a house.
~ Those who cannot get a mortgage.
~ Those who think they may be on the road to a divorce and who don't want to split or share the house with a future ex-spouse.
~ Those who have a house in one area but who work for a while in another part of the country.
~ Those who have a controlled, fixed or capped rent.

Sasha's story

My mother rented a flat as a temporary measure during the Second World War, but what with one thing and another (including two marriages and having me) this temporary arrangement lasted for 31 years. The flat was on a controlled rent that never increased, so eventually the rent was actually lower than her Council Tax bill. When developers moved in to replace the flats with an office block, my mum and step-dad bought a bungalow.

I know another person who has lived in a rent-controlled house for many years. The rent has gone up a little, but it is still less than a quarter of what other rentals would be.

Top tip

If you fall on hard times, the Income Support will help with your rent, but probably not the whole amount.

Our verdict

There are no new controlled rents, so get on the property ladder. However, don't be tempted to take out the biggest mortgage you can afford; make sure that if interest rates increase in a couple of years time, that you will be able to afford the repayments with rates at, say, 8%. Otherwise, get a fixed rate deal for five years or so.

And, if you just can't afford the deposit on even a chicken coop with today's high property prices, here's what to do: save up for a deposit anyway, because there is always the chance that property prices will drop, be it sharply or slowly, as they have many times before, after massive increases like those we have seen over the past few years. Don't be left without your deposit at the ready if this happens!

13

Insurance

The purpose of insurance is to put you back where you
were before you needed to claim for
whatever was insured.
Gwen Handy, previously of P. T. Cracknell Ltd., Insurance
Brokers.

You can insure almost anything, within limits. There is an advertisement running on the television these days for a hair product and the woman in the advert comments that there was once an actress who insured her legs for a million dollars. Well, you have to be pretty old to remember who the leggy actress was - but Sasha remembers, because her father was a great fan of the beauty in question. Her name was Betty Grable.

Insurance is useful and even essential in some cases, but it can be unnecessary and wasteful in others. When times are hard, you need to watch that you are not paying to insure the same bit of drain pipe on two different policies, but you don't want to be faced by a bill if something goes wrong, either.

Look around before you buy any type of insurance. The "direct" companies are less expensive than those that are attached to an organisation or that go through a broker, but the cover on a policy can vary widely from one organisation to another, so look closely at what you get for your money - there is sense in finding an *ethical* independent insurance broker, who will often know the answers to questions you may not think of asking.

To some extent, you can take recommendations or advice from sensible friends and relatives. For example, if someone has had a good result from a particular company, it is worth taking this on board. However, if your dad has always used a particular company, there is no reason why you should have to do the same. Always look around and always read the small print before you take out any policy.

Mortgage insurance

Your lender will probably insist on this. If he doesn't, then take it out anyway. Jan has known one family personally, where the father died in an accident and the wife was left homeless, as she couldn't keep up the heavy mortgage repayments on her own.

Life assurance

This is essential if a person is in the armed services or in a dangerous job, otherwise it is worth considering anyway. It can be expensive, so when hard times come it may be difficult to keep up the payments. However, you can usually stop payments and freeze the policy at the value applicable at the time. A life policy is also useful as security for a bank loan, once it has started to build up a *surrender value*. This is the name given to the value of the policy if it were to be cashed in, or surrendered.

Don't ever surrender a life policy unless there is absolutely no other alternative - rather than surrendering it, you may well be able to get a loan against the policy from the insurance company that issued it - the *loan value* will likely be a bit less than the surrender value, but you may not have to make any repayments at all until you can afford to do so again. At the same time, you still have a level of life cover, which you would lose if you surrendered the policy.

Insuring against illness, accident and injury
This kind of insurance is useful for those who are self-employed, and it is essential for those who do a physical or potentially dangerous job.

Public liability insurance
You should take out this kind of insurance if you work in any place where other people might get hurt (or hurt themselves).

Key worker insurance
This is only of interest to those who are in business, as you might want to insure yourself, a partner or some other person against them becoming so ill that they are unable to continue working.

Redundancy insurance

If you have a high-powered job that would take you time to replace if you were made redundant, redundancy insurance should cover you for a year or so while you look around for a new job. It can be expensive, so consider how necessary it is, before signing up.

Private medical insurance

This can be worthwhile if you can afford the payments. Private hospitals don't treat every kind of ailment - and while they all look very nice, the standard of care is not always as good as it would be in a National Health hospital. You can always pay a consultant for an initial examination out of your own pocket, so if that is all you want, insurance may be unnecessary. If you want more, you must compare what each company charges and what they offer.

Some companies insure for dental and optical treatment, others do not. All private insurers ask for your medical history and they may not pay out for an existing condition. The amount you pay for this insurance depends upon your health, your age and your lifestyle. There are plans that pay for full private treatment, plans that top up NHS treatment and many other variations on a theme on offer. The Internet is probably as good a place as any to start your search.

Insurance against the cost of going into an old people's home

This may well be a good idea, but it depends so much on individual circumstances that it is really essential to look into it with an independent financial advisor or someone qualified to guide you on the subject.

Insurance against having to pay Inheritance Tax

If your estate is worth more than £255,000 at the time of writing, your beneficiaries will have to pay IHT. You can insure against this, but the premiums are so high that you might be better off just putting some money aside for the IHT. Anyway, you won't be around to worry about it by then!

Insurance towards the cost of a funeral

This can be a rip-off in some cases. We don't recommend any particular firm as a rule in this book, but it is well known that the Co-op has had a funeral scheme for just on 150 years, so this is probably one of the best companies to insure with for this purpose. Otherwise, just put enough money aside for the kind of funeral you want and make your wishes known by writing them down when you make your will.

Buildings insurance

If you own a property, you have to insure it by law in case it falls down. This covers the structure of the building and anything that is integral to it, such as the loo, bath and windows. Some years ago, vandals threw a stone through one of Sasha's windows. Being a large double-glazed window, it would have been expensive to replace, but the buildings insurance paid for it. This is not an expensive form of insurance and it is vital. You are obliged to take this insurance when you take out a mortgage. Do ensure that your insurance is enough to cover the cost of rebuilding your house. It should rise a little year on year, if it is not enough you can ask to have it raised.

Contents insurance

There is bound to be some kind of accident or incident in a house at some point in time, so you must cover your household contents with this kind of insurance. Don't use a cowboy insurance company, even though the premiums will be lower than a better one. If you have jewellery and other stuff that you cart about with you, put these items on an all-claims policy so that you can be paid out wherever the loss occurs. You should increase this from time to time, but don't increase it to the point where the insurance company thinks you are about to set the house on fire and make a fraudulent claim.

Drains, gas, electricity and so on

Check your household buildings and contents policies to see what they cover. If they don't cover everything in the above list, then insure these items separately with your gas, electricity or water company. It is wise to insure your gas appliances so that you can have them serviced annually and checked for carbon monoxide emissions. When the gas man cometh, watch what he does. If he does no more than measure the emissions from your flu without servicing the boiler properly, phone the company while he is in your house and complain loudly.

Top tip

~   If you have to call in a builder or other tradesperson to
    do extensive work on your premises, ask to see their

insurances. They should be covered for public liability insurance, employer's liability insurance and a contractor's all risk cover.

~   They should also belong to the Master Builders' Association (MBA). If you cut corners in this respect, you run the risk of falling victim to a cowboy builder who may do a shoddy job that needs to be redone.

~   Whenever possible, get references from a couple of the builder's previous customers. If he can't or won't give you two previous customers' names to contact, then it is very likely that his work is not up to scratch, and you should beware!

Flooding insurance

Global warming is a fact of life, but this has some strange effects. We may or may not notice the weather being warmer than it was, but the sea and river levels will rise. If you live by the sea, on a river or on a flood plain, either move away now or look into the possibility of insuring against flooding. The problem is likely to get worse unless some really effective measures are taken, and you may find that insurance premiums rocket sky high, or the property may even become uninsurable. If you can, why not move somewhere safer before problems crystallise? It was not uncommon for banks in South Africa to turn down home loans for properties built below the area's fifty-year floodline. this may not always be the case here, but even if the bank is prepared to grant such a loan, you shouldn't take it... ask any home owner in a flood-stricken area whether he would buy such a property again!

Motor insurance

It is illegal to drive a vehicle without a valid insurance certificate. This must cover the basics of fire, theft and injury to other road users (third party). However, it is best to take out a fully comprehensive policy that covers everything and that allows you to drive someone else's vehicle on your own insurance in an emergency. Take a policy that includes a courtesy car, as this can be useful.

Breakdown insurance

This is essential if you do a lot of driving. Take out the insurance that allows someone to come to your vehicle whether it is on the road or even on your own front drive. You also need recovery cover so that you and your vehicle can be transported home.

Sasha's story

It was well known when I wrote for the Aquarian Press that I was a jinxed traveller, so it was with some trepidation that they sent me all over the country to do bookshop signings and other events. On one occasion, I was sent to a conference in Stratford upon Avon and I had to stay in a hotel over a weekend. My own car was such a wreck that Tony (my first husband) offered to lend me his nice, large, comfortable motor for the trip in case mine didn't make it, but I ended up wishing I had taken my faithful old banger.

When the time came for me to drive home, the car wouldn't start, and this was a very wet and cold February night. Various people tried starting the car with jump leads and so on, but no joy. Fortunately, Tony belonged to an automobile club, so I called them out. Eventually a little man trundled along and proceeded to look in the bonnet of the car. He tried all the obvious means of getting it to start but he couldn't get it going. He rather fancied messing around with this car, as it was a make and type that he rarely came across, and he started talking about taking the engine apart. By this time, I was cold, wet, very tired and somewhat hysterical, so I put a stop to this lunatic. I told him to call up the tow truck and get me and the car home. He reluctantly did so.

The next day, we asked our neighbour, who was a very good car mechanic, to come and take a look at the car. He saw immediately that two leads were touching each other and as soon as he moved them apart, the car started like a dream.

I wish to point out that I am in no way running down the automobile club here, and at the end of the day, this insurance did ensure that I got home that night. It was just that this particular employee was a prat!

Extended household appliance insurance

This is often a huge rip-off, because the money that is charged would buy you a new appliance - twice over in some cases. The one machine that is likely to conk out is the washing machine, because this does heavy work. Some of the plastic bits on a dishwasher can wear out, but these are not expensive to replace. It is far cheaper to get a machine fixed or even replace it altogether than to pay this extortionate insurance. Fridges and cookers can last at least twelve years if they are not interfered with. It is far better to put some money aside in case you have to replace these things.

Credit card insurance

Sentinel and other firms offer insurance for the loss of your credit cards, for fraudulent use of them by a thief, loss of your house keys and so on. This is worth it, but there is a strange catch here. Some credit card companies will offer this service free with your card, and you may well be able to get your firm to offer this too, if you phone and ask them, even though they don't make this known.

Credit card payment insurance

This insurance pays part of the interest on your credit cards bills. It can be very useful for those times when you might be sick or out of work, or when something else goes wrong. It probably won't cover the cost of all that you owe, but it helps.

Travel insurance

Always take this out when you travel. You can take insurance for a single trip or for multi-trips and you can do so as an individual, a couple or as a family. You can insure for a skiing holiday or many other normal sporting activities, but most insurance will not cover you for extreme sports. Look at the price and the small print on these policies. We have found that the Post Office insurance is good value and its cover is better than some far more expensive policies. Things can change, however, so always check around shortly before your trip.

One other thing to keep in mind - travel policies usually exclude business travel, unless you have specifically requested this cover. Don't assume your business trip is automatically covered!

Pet insurance

If you have pets, you should insure them, because vet's bills and your pet's medicines can be costly. Watch out for rip-offs here though, so compare prices and what is covered. We only have a hamster and we don't bother with insurance for him, but even he cost us a few pounds in veterinary bills when he went down with a cold and had to have antibiotics. I nearly needed to be insured for mental breakdown when I had to hang on to him twice a day so that Jan could get the medicine down his throat!

Top tips

A cheaper insurance company may take a longer time to service your claim and it may try to wriggle out of paying you the full amount – or indeed, anything at all.

Don't claim for every little mishap on your household insurance, because the premiums increase every time you make a claim, and there may be a limit to what the insurance company will put up with. It helps your premiums considerably if you can build up a few years worth of no-claim bonus.

Don't make malicious or frivolous claims. If you have an accident or a mishap, claim by all means, but don't make a nuisance of yourself by trying to screw the insurer; this always works against you in the long run, and you may well gain a black mark against your name, and become uninsurable.

14

Pension Plans

Spare when you are young and spend when you are old.
Proverb.

Here are three pieces of information that look as though
they should be true:

~ If we pay into the National Insurance scheme every
  week without fail from the time that we leave school
  until we retire, we can look forward to a state pension
  that will cover our basic needs of home, food and
  shelter, if not more than this.
~ Everybody should put as much as they can afford into a
  private pension plan for as long as possible, and then
  continue to pay into it for a few years longer if
  necessary, in order to obtain the greatest benefit from it.
~ Everybody should pay into a company pension scheme.

Are these statements true? Well yes... and no.

Think back over the years since you left school and consider the following questions:

~ Has you life gone in a smooth pattern and do you have an unbroken work record?
~ Will the State pension cover your basic needs?
~ Have you stayed with no more than one or two companies and earned substantial sums of money over the years?
~ Does your firm or organisation have a good, final salary, pension scheme? If so, will your final year's salary be high?
~ Has your marriage stood the test of time?
~ Is your private pension plan a good one and have you paid enough into it to make it worthwhile?
~ Can you be certain that you will never be made redundant?

We were listening to a radio programme the other day on the subject of early retirement. The commentator on the programme said that those who had retired (early or otherwise) in the 1970s and 80s were the first (and probably the last) generation who could give up working completely and hope to live on some kind of pension. He implied that, in future, we will probably have to go back to the way it was in the olden days. Then people did at least some light work for many years after the current retirement age, simply in order to survive.

The whole area of pensions is amazingly complicated and we can only skim over the surface in this chapter, but let us begin by taking a look at two lucky winners in the pension game.

Arthur's story

Arthur was a policeman. He stayed in "the job" until the normal police retirement age of 55, by which time he had reached the rank of Superintendent. Then he took a job as a security manager for a fast food chain until his official retirement age of 65. Arthur had always paid into the National Insurance scheme, he had paid the top up SERPS (State Earnings Related Pension Scheme) and he paid into the police super-annuation scheme. He paid into a pension with the fast food company. Arthur's wife, Gina, was a teacher. She had worked before having children and then went back to work once they were old enough for her to do so and she paid into the teacher's pension scheme. Arthur and Gina have had a long and happy marriage. Now they are retired. Their house is paid for, their children are happily settled and they garden, entertain, spend money in DIY stores and go on nice little cruises.

George's story

George worked for others for some years until he started his own business at the age of 42. He has always paid into the National Insurance scheme, including SERPS. He took out a private pension soon after starting his business and he increased the amount he has paid into this over the years. George's wife, Sarah, worked as an office administrator for most of their married life and she has paid into a company pension. Sarah also paid the full National Insurance contribution in addition to SERPS during that time. George and Sarah are now enjoying their timeshare in Florida, their golf and entertaining their friends and family.

Lucky Arthur and Gina. Lucky George and Sarah. Those of us who have lives that are filled with ups and downs that are likely to affect our pensions will have to think of something to afford us comfort in our old age. But what? The answer depends upon our age and stage in life, the future of the country, the nature of those who we work for, the stock market and many other unforeseen factors, but here are a few suggestions.

National Insurance contributions

Always pay the full National Insurance contribution including the SERPS (state earnings related pension scheme). If a pension seller suggests that you contract out of SERPS and to put the money into a private pension plan - don't listen.

If you are self-employed, you won't be able to pay SERPS, so you *should* pay this part of your contribution into your private plan.

If you are paying a married woman's "Certificate of Election", scrap this and start to pay the full contribution immediately. You should be able to top up your payments for the previous six years and you must do this now.

If you are a woman and you fall pregnant and are out of work before your first child is born, pay voluntary contributions until the birth of the child. You are covered until your last child reaches the age of 16. If you are out of work after your last child is 16, pay a voluntary contribution so that you keep up an unbroken a line of eligibility for benefits.

Get married when young and stay married to the same person forever. (Remember, this book is not about relationships, feelings, love, marriage vows, getting bored with your partner or having an exciting sex life: it is about money!)

A widow can benefit from her husband's SERPS payments, but a widower cannot benefit from his wife's. Be aware that on remarriage, a widow loses out on her late husband's pension and SERPS entitlements.

Even without doing the above, you should still receive some kind of basic pension, possibly topped up by Income Support. In future, the state pension is likely to be paid at an older age than it is now – possibly 65 for a woman and 70 for a man, so start saving – and start doing it now. Keep your eye on the situation via the brochures in the Post Office, the Benefits Office and the Internet.

The maximum state pension at the time of writing

As long as the man has paid contributions for a total of 44 years, he will receive the maximum pension. As long as a woman has contributed for a total of 39 years, she will receive the maximum pension in her own right. A woman with children will be covered for the whole period during which she had children under the age of 16.

A husband will receive the maximum pension of £75.50 per week and his wife will receive a further £45.20. If both partners have worked and paid the full amount, the woman will also receive £75.50, so they would then receive £151 per week between them. In addition, if either or both have earned good money during their lifetime and contributed to SERPS, they will receive a little more.

If a person contributes the full amount into the scheme for about a dozen years, he or she will receive some part of the state pension, but if the person has paid contributions for fewer years than this, he or she will receive nothing. If a woman has paid into the truly evil Certificate of Election scheme, she will get a stupid pittance such as seven pence per week, if she is lucky. Paying a reduced rate due to low earnings (but not the Certificate of Election) will count as a full contribution.

There are also some extras that are paid to pensions, such as a cold weather payment. This is supposed to arrive in January but it often doesn't do so until about the following May. The message here is not to rely on getting a state pension, especially one that you can live on. This situation will get worse in future, so some form of top up private pension or savings plan is essential.

State pension - Jim's story

Jim has had a spotty work record and he has been out of work for lengthy periods of time. Jim will not receive a full pension.

State pension - Anita's story

Anita left school at fifteen, worked and paid her National Insurance contributions. She married Dean when she was seventeen and she gave up work two years' later, when she and Dean had one child. Eventually Anita took a part time job. Her employer suggested that she sign the *Certificate of Election*. Anita assumed that the Certificate would contribute to a state pension, but neither the Certificate nor the Benefits Office pointed out to her that it only covered Anita for injury while at work. Eventually Anita took on full time work, so she telephoned the Benefits Agency to ask whether she should now pay a full contribution. The clerk told her not to bother as she could rely upon an extra payment off the back of Dean's payments.

Dean's normally unpleasant behaviour turned into full-blown abuse, so at the age of 52, Anita divorced Dean. A year later, she met Jack and remarried, but Jack died eight years' later. Jack had had a spotty payment record due to having lived abroad for many years. Anita received little or no state pension and had to rely on handouts from her daughter.

Company pensions

Company pension schemes used to be based on the final year's salary, so those who rose in the ranks of the company and earned good money in their last few years did very well. In some companies this is still the case, but some have found that they can no longer afford to pay full (or any) pensions. Some companies have gone bust. It would be churlish to suggest that this was because their finances were being crippled by the heavy pension burden, but it couldn't have helped. Many larger schemes have come unstuck purely because the trustees did not put aside enough reserves during good years, apparently thinking the good times would last forever. Another case for regulation - or rather, effective regulation, not just for the sake of red tape.

Redundancy

If you are made redundant and you have contributed to a company pension, see if you can move your scheme from your old company to a new one when you find another job.

There will be a penalty for doing this, but it is still worth trying to salvage something.

Private pension plans

Private pension schemes are a great idea, but they are hedged around with rules, regulations, fees, charges, problems and setbacks. The good thing is that the money that one pays into a pension scheme is offset by tax relief. The bad thing is that no one goes out to buy a pension plan - they are usually sold to you. The plan that is sold is wonderful for the agent because he receives as much as the first year's payments in commission, and perhaps also something on top of that throughout the plan.

You can arrange for your pension, or a portion of it, to be paid to your partner in the event of your death, but this lowers the amount payable to you throughout the life of the pension. Similarly, there are other options available, and these also affect the level of payments made to you.

When you retire, you can decide to take part of your pension (currently up to 25%) as a lump sum and leave the rest as a monthly pension, or you can use the whole sum to produce your monthly income. You can even defer the pension and keep on paying into it for longer than you had originally planned (current legislation limits this option to your seventy fifth birthday). You will need to read the small print on your plan and perhaps also to consult the company that issued the pension in the first place, to check their own specific terms and conditions.

If you are self-employed, you *must* pay into some kind of private pension plan or save in some other way. If your business fails and you have no income, you may not be allowed to continue with the pension plan, but you can still save in other ways. See if you can take a payment holiday or remain self-employed in some way (even if only on paper).

Top tip

~ Even if you are really strapped for cash, don't cancel or surrender pensions or life policies. See if you can take a payment holiday or at least reduce the payments for a while. You can also approach the insurance company for a loan against the "loan value" of a life policy. This keeps the policy alive while you have the benefit of a loan against it, and under more flexible conditions than a bank loan secured against your policy. A loan value usually accumulates from two years after inception of the policy. You should make every effort to at least repay interest on the loan, otherwise you'll see your policy slowly losing all its value.

~ Buying ISAs each year can work as a form of personal savings towards one's old age, as over the long term they should still work out better than many pension plans. Perhaps look at a tracker unit trust and drip feed savings into that over a period of years. The combination of these two activities will augment a poor State or company pension. At worst, they will provide you with at least some income when you get older.

Our verdict

Take lots of advice, talk to the Social Security people, read every brochure, article and book that you can find, and take care about how you invest. But, for heaven's sake, do *something* to secure your future in these uncertain times - and do it as soon as you can. Talk to two or three independent financial advisors, and use your common sense.

Living abroad

If you decide to spend your golden years overseas you may find that your pension is set at the level that it was when you left the UK and that it will not increase in the future. The situation is not as bad if you decide to live in the European Union as in some old Commonwealth countries. These are Canada, Hong Kong, South Africa, Zambia, Zimbabwe, New Zealand, Trinidad and Tobago. Some advice notes say that Australia is all right, others say that it is not, so check this one personally if it concerns you.

Bear in mind that even the EU situation may change in the future, and there is some talk of disparity between the systems here and in Spain and other places. So check this out if it applies to you, before you commit yourself to emigrating.

Annuities

Once your pension plan has reached its sell-by date, or when you decide to turn it in, you have to use at least 75% of it to purchase an annuity. The amount that you receive each month will then usually be fixed, depending on which type of annuity you buy. You definitely need expert advice about this because once purchased, you cannot change your mind about the annuity.

Timing is critical when purchasing an annuity, because they are mostly maintained through investment in the stock market. If the markets are poor, your annuity is likely to give you a poor return. It is usually possible to postpone taking up an annuity until you are seventy five years old, if necessary, and if you can afford to wait.

The other very important point to remember is that you are not obliged to purchase the annuity from the institution that administered your pension fund. You are strongly advised to look around, as there are often substantial differences in annuity benefits between different companies.

Any respectable independent broker will be happy to list a range of annuities from different insurance companies for you to consider, free of charge. There can be as much as 30 percent difference between the payout levels of some annuities, so look carefully into the choices available to you.

You will also have to take into account factors such as the following:

~ A straightforward annuity, fixed amount, payable to you for life.
~ Or, payable for life, then a portion or all of the pension payable to your spouse for a period, or for life.
~ A guaranteed payment for five or so years, even after death.
~ Inflation-linked annual increased payments.

All these options naturally vary the payout amounts (usually downward), as they are all sourced from the same basic pot of money you accumulated through your pension contributions.

One type of option that, unusually, increases your income from an annuity, is the "serious disease" option available from many insurance companies. In other words, if for example, you are a smoker, you are estimated to have a shorter life expectancy, so the insurance company feels it can pay you more, for a (probably) shorter period. Gruesome thoughts, maybe, but nevertheless, they must be considered, as you must make every effort to maximise your annuity benefits from the outset - you can not back out of your choices afterwards, and you can't change or cancel the annuity.

15

Energy Saving Tips

A small leak will sink a great ship.
Proverb.
We never miss the water until the well runs dry.
Proverb.

Marilyn was married to a very stingy guy who wouldn't allow her to turn the central heating on in the winter. She and their three small children walked around indoors huddled in their outdoor coats and they often had to go to bed just to keep warm. Two of the children became seriously ill and my friend spent a fortune running backwards and forwards to visit them in hospital. Ignoring the fact that this man's behaviour was both selfish and cruel, it also turned out to be expensive – not for him of course; he didn't bother to visit his sick children, but Marilyn struggled to cope with the cost. It was no surprise to anybody when Marilyn walked out of the marriage, taking her tight-fisted husband to the cleaners in the process. The moral of this true story is that saving energy is always a good idea, but not at the risk to your family's health or your own - or to your marriage.

Insulate for snugness

Take a look at your loft. If it has not been insulated, do it now. If there is insulation in place, check that it is at least 25 centimetres thick and if it insufficient; dump another layer on top.

You can cover exposed pipes with special polystyrene (Styrofoam) tubing that is cut open along its length and thus, easy to fit.

Fit an insulating jacket to your hot water tank. You will recoup the cost of this in under a year.

Check for local government grants that may be available for these basic measures and other energy saving devices.

A word for windows

If you can afford double-glazing, install it. Remember to get at least three quotations and look carefully at what you are buying.

Replace glass louvers with double glazed windows. Louvers aren't burglar proof and they waste heat.

Check for gaps around the edges of the windows where they meet the frames. You can fill these up by squirting flexible sealant into them. Do the same outdoors as well as inside.

If you can't afford double-glazing at the moment, buy plastic frames that click together and hold sheets of plastic glass. Measure your windows, get the plastic cut to fit and screw this temporary glazing in place. You can open these secondary windows or unhook them and put them away once the weather improves.

A quick-fix method comes in a pack that includes double-sided sticky tape and sheets of special polythene. Stick the tape around the window, cut the polythene to size and fit it in place, then use a hair-dryer to shrink the polythene into shape. Unfortunately, this leaves a residue on the window frames when it is removed, but it is worth using as a temporary measure if you intend to replace the windows and frames down the line. If you are in rented property, work out whether the landlords are likely to charge you for rubbing down and repainting the windows when you leave.

If your curtains are thin, change them or buy curtain linings and put them onto a separate track. Draw curtains once it gets dark.

Draughty floors and doors

Fill gaps around the skirting with beading, flexible sealant or by stuffing folded newspaper in them.

It is fashionable to have sanded floorboards rather than fitted carpet. This option is certainly much cheaper than carpet, but draughts will come up through the floor. Depending upon the age and condition of your floorboards, consider some other option.

On a cold evening, run your fingers all around the door edges. You will soon find the draughts. Then fit draught excluders to doors, especially the bit at the bottom of the door. Alternatively, buy or make a sausage shaped thingy and use that. The sausage can have another unexpected benefit. My friend's small dog spent many happy hours being amorous to the sausage – so it not only kept the draught out but it kept the dog happy at the same time!

In the old days, people used to put a curtain rail over a draughty door and hang a heavy lined curtain that could be pulled across. If you wish to resurrect this old idea, it isn't worth buying a good curtain, so look around in charity shops, boot or jumble sales for the right kind of heavy velveteen or damask curtain.

Fit a draught excluder or even a piece of carpet or curtaining over the back of a draughty letterbox flap in your front door.

Warnings

Blocking up every draught is all very well,but you need some oxygen and fresh air for health and safety.

Never block air vents under the house or elsewhere. Keep chimneys and flues swept. Install a carbon monoxide detector.

If you move into a house that has an open fire, get the chimney cleaned and checked out. You may need to put a new lining into the chimney. Sooty residue and dust can catch fire and burn your house down.

Your old boiler

This is not a reference to your mother-in-law but your gas appliance! An old boiler may waste energy, so update it to a new one. This could pay for itself in just over three years. Get any boiler properly serviced once a year.

Check gas and electricity supply prices in your area; some may be less expensive than others.

Without being as daft as the man in the true story at the start of this chapter, see if you can turn the central heating down a degree or two. Don't sit about in a T-shirt during the winter, plonk on a fleece or a jumper. Your granny probably advocated wearing a vest in cold weather, but nowadays a T-shirt can act as a vest, so wear one under a shirt. Put on a pair of socks, because it is amazing how much difference that makes.

Turn radiators off in rooms that are not being used.

There was once a British comedian who used to punctuate his jokes by yelling "Shut that door!" to some unseen person off the side of the stage. This tag line was a hangover from the days when rooms were heated by open fires, so if the door was left open, the heat from the fire quickly dissipated. Another old cry was "Close that bloody door, I'm not paying to heat the street!" These old sayings may be amusing to modern ears, but they have a point.

Air conditioning
If you are one of those people who feel the heat so much that you find it hard to sleep in the summer, buy a portable air conditioner for the bedroom and make some kind of outlet for it, then close the windows.

Bring some electricity into your life
Get your electric wiring checked out because old and faulty wiring is dangerous and inefficient. Rewiring a house is expensive, but it may be necessary.

Electric storage heaters heat up special bricks during the night and the bricks release the heat during the day. They are not warm enough for Jan and Sasha, but if you don't feel the cold much, they are economical.

Turn off lights in any room that you are not using, but leave a light on where there are stairs for the sake of safety. Turning lights on and off ages your lightbulbs more than the cost of the electricity used by leaving them on, so if you are dodging in and out, leave the light on. Inexpensive night lights are useful. These use minimal electricity, stay on all night and are safety features, especially for children and the elderly.

When the time comes to replace appliances such as refrigerators, dishwashers or washing machines, buy energy efficient ones. Also, if you are only washing a half-load, use the half-load or economy wash.

Don't leave your television or video on standby. Ditto computers, if you know you are not going to use them for some hours.

Anything that uses a motor eats electricity, so use a radiant electric fire rather than a fan heater. Turn fans and fan coolers off if you are leaving a room for a period of time.

Water, water, everywhere

If your water supply is metered, you will be conscious of your water consumption. Even if it is not metered, conservation is good for you and for the planet.

Fix leaky taps, because even a slight leak can use up an awful lot of water and small leaks rapidly get worse - they never get better unattended!. Use a plug rather than allowing water to run freely. Perhaps use a bowl for cooking and washing up.

Oddly enough, a dishwasher is a good idea. It uses less water than washing up by hand and the money you spend on dishwasher tablets, powder or liquid is balanced by the money you save on washing up liquid, tea cloths, kitchen towels and wear and tear on your hands.. And you save money and time by not having to wash piles of these things each week.

Save hand washing up until you have a bowlful.

Take a shower rather than bathing, as this uses less water. However, Jan and Sasha firmly believe that a bit of what you fancy does you good, so have a lovely soak if you want to relax and unwind.

Put lids on saucepans and turn the heat down once the water has boiled. This not only saves energy but it also preserves the vitamin C in vegetables.

You may have no choice but to use a tumble dryer. If so, neither over nor under fill it. If you have the option, hang clothes out to dry when possible.

Dry clothes indoors on a clotheshorse rather than on a radiator, so that the radiator can still heat the room and not damage your clothes with its extreme heat.

Don't boil more water in the kettle or in saucepans than you actually need.

16

Bargains, Good and Bad Deals

You cannot lose what you have never had.
17th century proverb.

The true definition of a bargain is an item that you have every intention of buying at full price - it is the same quality as the full price item, but it costs less than you had expected to pay

A tale of two anoraks

Jan fancied a decent looking black outdoor coat or perhaps some kind of smart black anorak. We looked around for something suitable, but we couldn't find what he wanted until the day that we decided to explore a nearby local town. Unbeknown to us, we turned up there on market day, so naturally we wandered around the stalls. Suddenly my eye was caught by a rail of men's clothing, where I noticed a rather smart looking black anorak at a very good price. Joy of joys, there were two designs that fitted Jan perfectly, so he bought them both. As it happens, the jackets are fine - but even if they don't last forever, it doesn't matter, because we paid so little for them.

False economy

Sam worked in the office of an engineering factory - and Sam was notoriously stingy. Part of his job was buying metal that was needed for the factory as cheaply as possible. This was fine in principle - but often the men discovered that the metal that they were asked to work on varied in thickness and that it was actually wavy in places! The men wasted time trying to cut round the bad bits and they also wasted metal. The men weren't daft, they could see that Sam's method of buying was false economy. Sam didn't like to listen to the opinions of others and the owners of the firm didn't take enough notice of what was going on. Needless to say, the firm eventually went bust – and all because Sam was too careful with the owners' money.

Calling all bargain hunters

We think you are perfectly capable of spotting a real bargain for yourself, but we will suggest a few areas where you can save money. Frankly, we could gather enough information for this chapter to make a book in itself, but we will confine ourselves to a few obvious ideas.

Vehicles

If you are thinking of changing your automobile, consider buying a nearly new one rather than a brand new one. An ordinary make of vehicle is less expensive to service than a fancy one.

Renting equipment

You can rent a television, video, DVD, a washing machine or a dishwasher. You can also rent building equipment, steam paint strippers and special diggers for the garden if you only have a one-off job to do. This can be a clever short-term arrangement, but over the long term, renting is not a good option. The following are both true stories.

Madeleine's television

Madeleine rented a television. Five years later, she still had the same television on the same rental agreement, which was costing her £260 a year. She didn't upgrade the TV, but simply went on paying for what was by now an obsolete machine. As far as we know, she is still renting her telly.

A tale of two televisions

Jessica's mum was in a residential home for the elderly and one day the old lady's beloved telly went phut. Knowing that her mum depended on the TV for entertainment and news (her mother's eyes were no longer strong enough for her to read a newspaper), Jessica bought a good quality second hand set with a large screen and a really clear picture at just over £100. Her mum was ecstatic with her new set. While Jessica was scouting around for her mother, she decided that she could do with small television for her own kitchen, so she bought an excellent small set for herself at £39. The total cost for these two great sets was much less than Madeleine pays for a year's rental!

Setting up a home or setting up a home office

If you are setting up a home on a shoestring, some second hand furniture, televisions, CDs, telephones and so forth can be a real bargain. You can always replace these items with new ones later. This is even more so if you are setting up an office at home, because second-hand office furniture does the job just as well and it will save you a fortune.

Computers

A less expensive or second-hand computer might do what you want as well as a new one. We have to buy computers on a fairly frequent basis because they are central to our work, and we have been extremely disappointed with the newer ones and some of the latest software. If your old machine is still going strong, add some extra memory if necessary and carry on using it for as long as possible. Upgraded machines are increasingly complex and they aren't always all they are cracked up to be. A new computer itself is never the end of the story as the chances are that you will have to renew or upgrade your software as well – and that is far more costly than the replacement machine itself.

Electrical appliances

We have come to the conclusion that many shops sell extended warranties for the sole purpose of making money. As long as you take care with your appliances, most will last for many years. Those that are most likely to go wrong are the ones with moving parts, such as a washing machine, tumble dryer or dishwasher. With care, a decent model should last at least seven years, possibly more if it is not used too heavily. It will be cheaper and more satisfactory in the long run to mend or replace a worn appliance than to pay this insurance and some warranties won't even cover you for what you think they will. Can you be sure that you will still be living in the same area in a few years' time?

The only thing you can be sure of is that you will still have to pay for the extended warranty. It is far less expensive to insure yourself by putting money by so that you can replace such items when it becomes necessary.

Naturally, stick to well-known, reputable brand names - they have a reputation to maintain, so they are unlikely to sell shoddy goods.

A baby's goods

The baby soon grows beyond each stage and you don't use things like high chairs and so on for very long, so second hand items are often an excellent purchase. If the items are in good condition when you have finished with them, you can sell them on. If necessary you can buy second hand toys to fill in the boring gaps between Christmas and birthdays, or if your child is sick and in need of cheering up.

Shop in less expensive areas

Our children live near London, but we live in the West Country. When they visit us, they stock up on clothes and household goods because prices here are much cheaper.

Second hand goods, flea markets and boot sales

If you are setting up a home on a shoestring, you can buy second hand furniture and then replace it with new items, bit by bit, when you can afford to do so. Where small household items are concerned, a simply cracking idea is to find out where your local boot sale or flea market takes place and take a walk around there each week.

Conversely, when you want to clear some of the clutter from your home, you can rent a space at the boot sale and sell what you no longer need. Even if you only make enough money to take yourself and your loved ones out for a good meal or a day at the zoo, it is worth it, and it is fun to do. Charity shops are groaning with goods and they can be quite fussy about what they will and won't take. If you are short of money, be your own charity, and sell your clutter at a boot sale.

A few money saving wheezes

~ Don't try to keep up with the Jones's; you don't want their debts.

~ Work out whether you can do without cable, satellite or digital television for a while.

~ Rent videos for the family rather than visiting the cinema until things pick up again.

~ Cut your visits to the pub or social club from three times a week to two.

~ Don't eat out or buy takeaways so often and avoid processed and packaged foods. Cooking is tiring after doing a day's work but it does save money.

~ Take a packed lunch to work.

~ Use public transport if it works out to be less expensive than using a pay and display car park or parking meters in addition to petrol.

~ Use buses in preference to taxis or minicabs.

~ Find some inexpensive entertainment such as taking the children swimming. Perhaps take up line dancing with a friend, as this is fun and it doesn't require any special clothing.

~ Check out the local council, adult education centre and other subsidised ways of playing sport or getting fit.

~ Play pitch and putt. It is great exercise, children love it and it costs next to nothing.

~ If you use washing powder, don't fill the space in your washing machine with it, but experiment and see how much you really need to use.

~ Look around for a last minute bargain holiday if this is possible.

~ Don't spend money to make yourself feel good; you will end up feeling worse than before when the bills arrive.

~ If you are lusting after a Prada, Tod or LV bag (if you don't know what these are, you don't lust on the same scale as Sasha does); perhaps you fancy some Jimmy Choo's or Manolo's (ditto the LV handbag). If you must lust after any of these things, visit the second-hand and charity shops in a posh area. You will pay a fraction of the price, but you can still walk around with a smirk on your face. You mustn't let the cat out of the bag though, if you want people to think that you paid top dollar.

Clothes and the closet

It is an amazing fact that men and women who love to buy lots of expensive clothing are often less than clever about looking after them. Jamming clothes into a wardrobe or squashing them into drawers will ruin them, and the same goes for jumbling shoes into a heap. If you don't have enough hanging space, buy one of those mobile rails with a cover that goes over it and buy racks to keep shoes on. Never do housework in good clothes and never put dirty clothes away with clean ones. Fix loose hems and loose buttons. A set of plastic drawers from a DIY store or a stationery store is ideal to keep underwear, odds and ends, toiletries and cosmetics in.

Margaret Thatcher grew up in tight circumstances, so she always took care of her clothes. She even instructed the person who ironed her clothes never to iron her skirts right to the edge of the hems. This meant that if the fashion changed and the outfit needed to be lengthened or shortened, it could be altered without leaving a mark. You may not wish to go that far, but if you have a few expensive items that you intend to keep for some years, perhaps it is not such a bad idea.

Many years ago, when Sasha and her friends had small children and little money, they pooled some of their holiday clothes and shared them. One year, the same pool of clothes went to Spain three times in a row! Children's clothes can be passed on or shared in this way.

Don't toss out paper bags, elastic bands, paper clips and other odds and ends.

Don't bother to save on the following

~ Don't buy cheap and nasty food.
~ Don't buy inexpensive washing up liquid or bleach, because you will use more to get the same result.
~ Only use what you need rather than splashing it around willy-nilly. This may seem penny pinching, but it is amazing how such economies can help.
~ Don't use plastic shopping bags for storing foodstuffs.

~ Never put dangerous chemicals in a coke or lemonade bottle, because children may drink it by mistake.

~ And finally…cheap and nasty loo-rolls are false economy – for all kinds of reasons!

Is this a good idea?

We have recently come across an advert for a catalogue originating in America, called "The Pound-Saver Catalogue". Apparently this is full of money saving tips and ideas on how to use normal household products such as salt, vinegar and bicarbonate of soda rather than buying expensive specialised ones. It looks as though it is full of very clever ideas and it is available through Rodale Health Books, P.O. Box 2333, Swindon, SN3 4WG. We have not signed up for this, so we don't know whether it is worth having or not – and of course, it means spending money on the catalogue each month. We leave this one up to you.

When is a freebie not a freebie?

These days, magazines and newspapers are stuffed with adverts offering deals of one kind or another and they tumble through our letterboxes like confetti. If you receive a coupon for a reduction in price or a bogof (Buy One and Get One Free) for something that you would normally buy in that particular shop, it may be worth it. However, we find that trailing around the shops and looking for the item wastes more time, energy and petrol than we can spare. Some offers are designed to get your name on a mailing list, while others land you with a salesman coming to your house and pestering you.

A scratch card or anything else that tells you that you have won a free holiday should offer just that, but these things are often not free. At best, there will be a hefty "administration fee" for your free holiday. At worst, this will be a way of getting you to a high-pressure sales meeting for a dubious holiday club or a timeshare that you don't want and that you cannot afford. And you'll probably end up on another mailing list!

Cynical people exist to prey on those who answer their advertisements for pyramid selling (send £10 and you will get £100,000 back, earn by recruiting others, etc.), or buy an agency to sell some product. Some of these people prey on those who need money. The basic pyramid selling system is one where you supposedly earn more money by enlisting others than by selling the product, but there are many clever variations on the theme. Don't even think about doing anything of this kind.

Frankly, if you are really strapped for cash, apart from using the occasional coupon for a food item or a toiletry, it is best to shove all such brochures, leaflets, coupons and so on into your recycling bin. At least, that way you won't be tempted into spending money that you don't have on the latest scam.

Ignore all letters that show that you have been pre-selected for something or that you have won an award. One prize that we saw recently came to the glorious sum of £5 if you bought insurance from the firm in question and another offered a £15 bonus for signing up to a catalogue. This is pathetic.

If you like reading books from Readers Digest, buy them by all means, but don't think you will necessarily win one of their highly advertised prizes. We have been amused by recent television adverts from such organisations assuring people that they do have real prizewinners – is this because people don't believe that any prizes are really won? Do you *know* anyone who has ever won such a prize, from any such organisations? Sasha's first husband once won a bookmark from Readers Digest, so perhaps too much is made of a *very* few large prizes, whereas it would seem that most people can expect nothing. This is the same criticism that has been levied at the National Lottery (or Lotto, as it is now known), and hopefully things might change in future. Meanwhile, don't place too much hope on your saturday night ticket coming up...

Other nuisances

There are vast armies of people who go door-to-door to try to persuade people into changing their gas and electricity company or to buy some product or service. These people usually tell you that they are not selling anything, but they are! They can become very aggressive and quite frightening when you tell them that you aren't interested in what they have to sell. We have put a stop to this by putting a notice on our door. Even so, one guy still tried it on and he persisted until we threatened to call the police. Do the same if you don't wish to be bothered by these nuisance callers. If you like to buy some things this way (e.g. Betterware or Avon) you can put a note on the door asking them to leave a brochure for you to look at. These firms are fine, it is the pressure sales people who are a pain in the neck.

Never buy anything over the telephone. If you keep telling telephone sales people that you are not interested in their product, the number and frequency of calls drops off after a while.

Never respond to unsolicited faxes, even to try to cancel the junk. Once they know they have an active fax number, they will never let you alone, and will pass your number on to their mates.

Email junk mail

Don't respond to junk emails, don't even open them, don't buy from them. Don't be tempted to open unexpected, tempting emails from people you've never heard of. You will not get to spend the night with a sultry Russian princess, the cheap Viagra will most likely be a scam of some sort, and you may well end up with a computer virus for your curiosity. Just delete the messages, unopened. If they really get you down, email M*cr*s*ft and ask whether they spend more money on piracy protection and locking you in to them, or on virus-protecting their software. Jan actually likes (liked?) M*cr*s*ft software, but just cannot spend the time and energy worrying when the next Outlook virus / hacker problem is going to crop up. So, he uses other software wherever possible, that isn't as hot a target.

Scams

There are thousands of ingenious scams, and the television watchdog programmes make fascinating viewing. There was one terrific one in the paper recently where an estate agent was prosecuted under the Trades Descriptions Act for selling a property on the false premise that some royal personage had owned it or lived in it.

Finally...

Keep your bag zipped shut while you are out shopping. Don't leave purses, wallets, mobile phones or bags anywhere where a light-fingered person can snatch them. If you are in a pub or restaurant and you want to put your bag on the floor, put the leg of your chair through the handle. Also, keep your pin number shielded while you are at a cash point. If anything untoward happens, inform the card company immediately.

17

Wills and Inheritance Tax

Making a will doesn't mean that you are preparing to die; it just means that you are being sensible. The same principle applies to life assurance policies. In both cases, everyone knows that they will die - eventually - but no-one knows *when* they will die. If you leave a properly witnessed will, preferably one that has been drawn up by a solicitor, then your family won't have to hang around for years in a state of financial insecurity. If you take a mortgage, take the kind of mortgage insurance that pays for the house if you die suddenly. Remember the story about Ann and Gus, and how he had taken this at a time when it was unusual to do so. This meant that Ann didn't have to cope with being thrown out on the street with her two children, on top of all her other worries and miseries at that time.

If you are a beneficiary of someone else's will, bear in mind that at best, it could easily be eighteen months before you get paid out. Even long after this, stray bills could come in, so you should put part of the legacy away for this purpose. If you are the executor of a will, you will be signing papers and dealing with things for a couple of years after the person's death.

Inheritance tax (IHT) used to be the province of the very rich, but now it affects many ordinary people. At the time of writing, IHT is levied on that part of a person's estate that is over £255,000. A perfectly ordinary house can easily sell for this kind of money, so it is clear that many people will get caught up in this one. Take advice if you need it, as there may be ways of minimising this tax. For instance, you should put your home in both your name and that of your partner, because the value of it will then be shared. There is no IHT between married partners, so if you are not actually married to your long-term lover, this might be the time to think about having a nice little wedding.

This important point applies to pensions and many other critical issues; the current vogue of just living together may be cool and cocking a snoot at the establishment, but individuals can suffer badly - especially women - unless they are married.

We don't have space here to discuss the pros and cons, but we have one, purposely exaggerated, thought for those (men?) who scoff at marriage - if you're in an accident that leaves you in a coma and the hospital thinks that amputating your willy may save your life, your unmarried partner can't tell them no! Far-fetched examples aside, unmarried partners are not next-of-kin, do not automatically inherit anything, have no say in hospital or elsewhere and generally have no more rights in the eyes of the law than a stranger off the street. Changes are afoot to ease this kind of problem for gays and their partners, but no such changes are likely for unmarried heterosexuals. Why? Because they already have the marriage option available, which solves the problem completely.

Top tip

~   Don't make a family member or a friend the sole executor of your will. This can work well enough when a solicitor is the co-executor, but it can make enemies within the family if the relative is the sole executor.

18

Taxation

Laws grind the poor and rich men rule the law.
Oliver Goldsmith.

Even if you live on benefits and never pay income tax, you certainly do pay tax each time you go out and buy something and on every bill that you pay. Tax is levied in the form of Income Tax, Capital Gains Tax, National Insurance, Value Added Tax, Inheritance Tax, stamp duty on a house purchase, extra taxes on fuel such as petrol, pensions, cigarettes and alcohol and other things. It is true that income tax has been held steady (so far), as claimed by the government, but a lot of indirect taxation has cropped up in the last few years. We are not political types, simply observant of what goes on, whichever party is in power.

One of the few things that are not taxed in any way is a book (so far) - so buying this one represents a real bargain!

Pay As Your Earn (PAYE)

We all know what this one is; it is the tax that is taken out of your pay packet before you receive your salary or wages. National Insurance contributions are also taken in this way. If you take a new job, you will be put on to emergency tax for a while until your true tax situation is worked out. Emergency tax is usually on the high side, so when this is sorted out, you can usually expect to receive an extra large pay packet which includes the tax rebate.

Annual taxation

If you earn a lot of money in any particular year and if you earn interest on savings and investments, you may find that you receive some kind of extra tax and NI bill a couple of years later. It is wise to put something away for this eventuality.

Self employed people and those who own businesses are taxed on an annual basis. If your affairs are simple, you may be able to manage the tax form yourself, and you can make an appointment to see someone at the Inland Revenue who will help you with this. In this case, take all notes and documentation about your circumstances with you to the meeting. If your affairs are more complicated or your business is more involved, you will need an accountant. The downside is that accountants cost money – and you will still have a tax bill to face somewhere along the line. The upside is that a good accountant can save you from paying unnecessary tax and he can claim rebates that are due to you. The Inland Revenue used to be less likely to investigate you if you have an accountant. Now they go after anybody, regardless of whether they use an accountant or not, so you might wish to take out insurance against this eventuality. The biggest problem is that the tax bill won't come along at a time when you are flush with funds, but a couple of years later when you are strung out. You must calculate your potential tax bill and put that money away in an account that you don't touch.

Although we are not going into small business ownership in this book in detail, there is one mistake that all people who are new to the business scene make, especially if they have been used to earning a salary as an employee. Even Jan got this one confused when he first went into business. If you are self-employed or if you own a private business (one that is not yet a limited company), your income is not just the money that you draw out of the business for your own living expenses. It is the *entire profit* of the business – and this applies whether part of it has been drawn or whether you live on something else and leave the profits in the business. Naturally, losses can be put against tax, and these can often be rolled forward over several years. You really do need an accountant for this type of situation.

Capital gains tax (CGT)

If you have more than one property and you sell one that is not your main dwelling place, if it makes a profit of more than £7,000, you will have to pay capital gains tax. A married couple with more than one property will pay CGT on a profit of more than £14,000. The tax is 40% of the extra profit. Naturally, this doesn't apply if you only own one property. There may be loopholes that apply to your home as opposed to a property that you use as a holiday home or that you rent out.

CGT can be levied on the sale of a business, on a profit on shares, on the sale of jewellery and antiques on several other things as well. For example, if you have worked from home for many years and routinely put a part of your home against tax, there may be a CGT bill to face when you come to sell the property. In all these cases, advice will be needed.

Value Added Tax (VAT)

VAT is levied at the moment at a rate of 17.5% on many goods and services. Fuel bills are levied at a lower rate (a quick look at our gas bill shows this to be 5%). Some items are zero rated, which means that they could become taxable at a later date. For example, books and the cost of printing them are zero-rated. Some things are exempt and will never be taxed. If you need to know more about VAT, you can borrow a book on this from the library, try the Internet or get in touch with HM Customs and Excise.

Inheritance tax

This was once the province of the very rich, but now it affects ordinary people, due to the sharp rise in the price and value of property. At the time of writing, an estate of more than £255,000 will fall into this category and any monies over this amount will be taxed at a rate of 40%.

National Insurance

Everybody who earns money pays NI. If your earnings in any particular year are below a certain level, you can pay a smaller amount of NI but still claim benefits and pensions.

Taxation is a large and complicated matter, so we have only covered the basics in this book. If you have any problems, consult the Inland Revenue, the Citizens Advice Bureau or get a really good accountant on recommendation. We can recommend our London accountant because we have found him to be careful, helpful and very professional. His firm, Howard S Markham & Company, is in Hampstead, London, he doesn't overcharge and his advice has saved us thousands of pounds.

email:– email@howardsmarkham.co.uk

How about that; perhaps we should ring Howard and ask him to sponsor a page or two in our book!

19

Divorce and Separation

A great dowry is a bed full of brambles.
Proverb.

Any solicitor will tell you that most people are much
poorer after a divorce than before. Almost half those who
marry part company down the line, and the practical
problems that follow a divorce will be worse during
uncertain times than in good ones. It is usually the woman
who takes the financial brunt of a divorce (yes, really) and
who usually has take care of the children in addition to
looking after herself. The following questions are
somewhat biased towards women, but some will apply to
both parties, and even by extension to subsequent partners.

The home

~ Will one of the partners continue to live in the marriage
home?

~ Can the husband afford to keep them in their present house – and will he?

~ What if the house has to be sold?

~ How much equity (money) is there in the house after the mortgage has been repaid, and is there enough for both parties to put a deposit on new homes?

~ Can either partner leave the area and live in a cheaper area?

~ Is there another person or persons involved? If there is, how will this person impact on the situation?

~ What if the husband starts another family? Will he still be able to pay maintenance at the same level?

~ What if the boyfriend turns out to be useless as a supporter?

~ Can the woman fix something in a house if it goes wrong? A friend of ours had to spend an hour squatting in deep snow in the street outside her house at four o'clock one morning while struggling to turn off a frozen stopcock!

~ Can the woman deal with bills and paperwork?

~ Can she get a man in to do some work in the home, ensure that the job is done properly and for the right price? There was recently a television programme about a gas company that took the annual insurance for man to check the boiler and gas appliances, but when the man came round he only measured the carbon monoxide emissions from the flue and didn't even look at the boiler. If a boiler has rust spots inside its casing, it could be on the point of filling the home with invisible, unscented fumes that can kill. Who would understand what was going on here?

~ If the woman hasn't worked for several years, what can she do to earn money? Has she skills or qualifications that will earn her a decent living?

~ If her skills are outdated and rusty, what can she do to update them or obtain new ones?

~ Will her income cover the cost of childcare? Even school age children are only at school for 32 weeks in the year at best. Children often catch colds or childhood ailments as soon as they go back to school, and they are more likely to be off sick during term time. Schools can suddenly close for a day with little or no warning.

~ Does she have the energy for a full time job, fetching children from a minder, cooking cleaning, shopping, mending things and getting stuff that the children need at the last minute completely unaided?

~ How many things does the husband do that she would have to do herself? I.e. fix the car, carry heavy things around?

~ What if she falls ill?

Money

Fortunately the days when men said "don't worry your pretty little head about these things" have vanished, but even now, there are situations where the man is considered to be the head of the house (especially ethnic marriages), and even in an English marriage where the man is strong-minded or much older than his wife.

~ Can she morph (change) overnight from someone who prided herself on nothing more than her clean windows and great dinner party skills into a financial wizard?

~ Can she cope if the husband doesn't help to support their children financially?

~ Could she face contacting the Child Support Agency?

~ Could she manage to live during the period before any money started to come through?

~ Would she need to go to the Social Services?

~ Does she know the family's tax situation?

~ Does she know how to find out how she stands legally?

~ Can she choose, buy, tax, insure, fix and run her own car?

~ Can she ask for a loan and not get caught up in one that is a complete rip off?

~ Can she face taking the children away on holiday on her own or does she have friends and relatives with whom she can travel?

How she copes with all this depends upon a host of variables, including such things as her personality and her experience of life before and during marriage. Also, whether she has a supportive family and friends, her ethnicity, where and how she lives and the money that is available to the post-divorce couple. She may be able to cope with all these things – or she may not.

Even consulting a solicitor to discover where she might stand if she were to decide to make the break is a big step for some women to contemplate. If you visit a solicitor for any reason, make notes about your situation and take them along. You must avoid becoming emotional or yakking at the solicitor about how badly you husband behaves or how unhappy you are. Time is money when you consult a professional and they charge by the hour, so emotional offloading should be kept out of the picture. Maybe visit the Citizens Advice Bureau as a starting point, as this is free of charge.

Keep notes of anything relevant to the case throughout the run up to a divorce and for some years afterwards. If you are thinking of splitting from your partner, give this at least as much thought as you did while planning your wedding or as though you were contemplating starting a small business.

Catherine

Catherine left her husband after he had carried on a spectacularly sleazy affair. They had no children and there was sufficient money in the pot for both of them to buy a home and live in a reasonable condition after splitting up. Catherine was interested in houses, and she had the skill to do them up and sell them on at a profit. However, she didn't have the money to get builders in to do the work so, despite being all of five feet nothing - and eight stone wringing wet, Catherine taught herself how to do this work and she developed a few muscles as a result.

Marjorie

Marjorie became disenchanted with her stingy and boring husband. They settled on one of those horrid arrangements where each lived in part of the house, used the kitchen and bathroom at different times and had little to do with each other. Neither wanted to give up the house or suffer the financial consequences of a divorce, so both dated other people and they lived like house sharers.

Men and divorce

A divorced man will lose some of the money that he has put into a previous home and he may then find it hard to finance his own needs, let alone to finance a second family. The Child Support Agency (CSA) will come after him even if he chucks his job and refuses to take any interest in his family. If he takes a new job, they will garnishee (take) some of his wages before he receives them. He may have to moonlight in an extra job just to make ends meet.

Life may be better after a divorce from an emotional point of view, but it is only better from a financial angle if the man leaves a truly spendthrift wife – and then only after a period of consolidation. Here is an astonishing story that is absolutely true.

Mike

Mike married twice. His first marriage foundered fairly early on, but he stayed with his wife while the children were growing up. Eventually he left and then married for a second time. His second wife was good with the children, but she was a real spendthrift. Mike was not stingy, stupid or lazy and his wife also worked - but she could spend money faster than they could earn it. Mike was far from being a controlling man, but there came a point one day when he cut up her credit cards - however, she found ways of getting new ones. Finally, the marriage fell apart. Like many people who have become exhausted by the trials and tribulations of a failed marriage, he walked out and left her with their house, but the situation left him broke and with debts hanging around his neck.

Mike took a day job as a salesman but he took a second job three evenings a week. He had previously spent some years in the army and he was still involved as a Territorial soldier, so he took over the running of the small regimental shop on an army base. The officers allowed him to live quietly in the back of the shop, to use the army's showers, and to buy meals in the NAAFI. He spent three years like this, sleeping on a camp bed at the back of the shop and heating bits of food on a camping stove. Mike never complained about this because he was glad for the army's unofficial help. Eventually, he cleared his debts and could rent a home.

Several years later, his ex-wife came to see him. She had spent all the remaining money, and the house and contents were being taken in lieu of payment for debts. She asked Mike to help her but he couldn't. Understandably, he wouldn't have helped her even if he could. These days, Mike dates women from time to time, but he has not become seriously involved with any of them.

Mike suffered from this divorce, but he stayed in work, took responsibility for his problems and kept in touch with his (then) adult children. Mike never had a drinking problem or anything else that made him unemployable or unacceptable.

Divorce may be easier for those whose children are old enough to be off-hand, but in some ways it is also harder. As we said earlier in this chapter, it all needs a lot of thought and consideration and a balance must be struck between living in misery and flouncing out just because the marriage has become boring or irritating. Only the parties themselves can work this out, at this time when uncertainty is looming over the horizon.

Women must take care of their pension requirements. An ex-wife may be able to claim on the husband's payments (state or otherwise) as long as she doesn't remarry. Naturally, if the couple were not married in the first place, this is not the case, the woman just doesn't get anything.

A man or woman may turn out to have no claim on the house. With or without being married, a partner may have no claim on what they spent the house, on furniture, appliances, soft furnishings and so on. In any dodgy relationship situation, it is wise to keep all receipts, cheque stubs, bank, credit card and other statements and be sure to cross reference these as proof. Cross-referencing is a bookkeeping term that involves linking each payment to its receipt by giving both a matching code number. Thus the first payment might be 001, the next 002 and so on.

Sometimes, the emotional damage of staying in a marriage outweighs even our suggestions. In the words of my friend, Anne, "It's nothing that a good divorce won't cure!"

20

State Benefits

Some people are entitled to help but they don't realise it, while others are too ashamed or too proud to ask. Here are a few situations that can land you in a mess.

~ Losing your job.
~ Getting into debt.
~ Becoming homeless.
~ Becoming pregnant.
~ One of your loved ones is unexpectedly pregnant.
~ Getting old.
~ Getting sick.
~ A partner suddenly leaving.

Even recent immigrants need help and advice.

You may be entitled to Child Tax Credit, Working Families Tax Credit or Working Tax Credit, Income Support or some other benefit. Don't sit about thinking that you can claim sums a couple of years down the line, you usually only have a few weeks available for you to get on to the system. It is often some time before you receive any money because these things take some time to come through.

If you are a pregnant teenager or if you have one in your house, you need to claim Working Tax Credit, Child Tax Credit, Housing Benefit, Maternity Grant, Milk Tokens, Income Support, Job Seekers Allowance and perhaps a Bridging Allowance. There are also many training schemes that are designed to equip the teenager with the skills required to earn a living in the future. This is just one area where help is available, but there are many others. For example, if you are starting a small business, you can pay a reduced National Insurance Contribution that still entitles you to all the usual health and pension benefits down the line and you may even be able to claim a Working Tax Credit while your business is getting on its feet. An older person can get disability allowances or Income Support to top up a pension.

We are all aware that there are people who abuse the systems because newspapers rush to tell us about it, but many of those who most need help don't ask for it. So, if for any reason you are struggling to survive, start to make enquiries. In this book, we will not go into the many and varied benefits that are available and we won't be able to give you the phone numbers or details of the various agencies. This is because our book is not about this area of finance - even if it were about benefits, we would probably need to update the book every few months.

Try the Citizens Advice Bureau, the local housing benefit shop, the local high street law shop, the Benefits Office, the Inland Revenue, your church or other religious institution, or friends who are in a similar position. Pop into the post office and pick up the booklets on the various kinds of benefits. Some of the advice that you will get will conflict and some will be out of date, but you will start to build up a picture of what is available and what you are entitled to.

Even charities can help, sometimes by offering advice and sometimes in a more direct manner. Nobody wants to become a charity case, but why should those who like to give money always hand it out to starving Africans? It appears that Africa will always tend to starve, because its corruption and tragic wars ensure this. We all know by now that the money is far less likely to reach that poor pathetic child whose photograph gets people to empty their pockets and pay for someone's new bullet-proof Mercedes or a presidential aircraft. Why not help those in Britain and then accept help yourself during those times when you need it? It is good karma for people to give, and it is good karma to take, because then you are then contributing to someone else's chance of building up brownie points in the karma department!

21 Index

A

B

Zambezi Publishing Ltd
"Much more than just books..."

All our books are available from good bookshops
throughout the UK; many are available in the USA,
sometimes under different titles and ISBNs used by our
USA co-publisher, Sterling Publishing Co, Inc.

Please note:-
Nowadays, no bookshop can hope to carry in stock more
than a fraction of the books produced each year (over
200,000 new titles are released in the Uk each year!).
However, most UK bookshops can now easily order and
supply titles within a matter of days, either from our
distributor (Airlift Book Company) or from us direct.
Alternatively, you can find all our books on
www.amazon.co.uk.

~~~~~

If you still have any difficulty in sourcing one of our
titles, then contact us at:-
Zambezi Publishing Ltd
P.O. Box 221, Plymouth
Devon PLY2 2EQ (UK)
Fax: +44 (0)1752 350 453
web: www.zampub.com   email: info@zampub.com
*You are also welcome to purchase our books direct
from our webshop at www.zampub.com*